According To Law
A Detective's Memoir

John Dee

Published by New Generation Publishing in 2021

Copyright © John Dee 2021

First Edition

ISBN

	Paperback	978-1-80369-130-5
	Hardback	978-1-80369-131-2

www.newgeneration-publishing.com

 New Generation Publishing

This book is dedicated to serving and retired police officers everywhere and especially to those with whom I worked. Many are no longer with us, including my good friends Phil Lawrence and Colin Merricks, both excellent detectives too soon losing their lives to cancer.

Author's Note

Although all events described in the book took place, some details, including names, dates and locations, have been changed.

Proceeds from the sale of this book are being donated to Cancer Research.

Contents

Preface

The original idea of writing this book came on retiring from the police in 2002 at the age of fifty-five. I reflected that the detail of many of the things that had happened over my thirty-six years of service might be of interest to my children as well as creating some sort of a career record to look back on. It also occurred to me that the story of how I came to join the police – and lessons learned on the way – might be of significance to others.

However, a combination of part-time employment as a civilian investigator and enjoying myself as a film and television extra, plus a few holidays, kept me otherwise occupied with little time to dedicate to writing a book. In 2008, doctors found a large mass blocking my bowel which turned out to be a stage three cancerous tumour, but the amazing National Health Service, not for the first time, came through for me and I was able to continue my life as before, albeit with a different perspective. The days became more valuable than they were pre-cancer, time with my family was a priority and birdsong and sunshine were properly appreciated. I still wanted to write the book but I knew it would be a lengthy process requiring plenty of commitment and patience. Not knowing if my cancer would return, I resolved to enjoy life as much as possible and to revisit the book project at a later time.

In 2011, I was told I had leukaemia. Not curable they said, but hopefully manageable. So, once more going through the stages of shock, fear and then acceptance of an uncertain future, the NHS cavalry came again to my rescue. Although on tablet chemotherapy, presumably for life, I am fortunate to have few side effects and able to continue a relatively normal existence. Family, birdsong and sunshine really are what life is about.

I thought once more about the book but again it was going to be a balance between allocating the time it needed against all that was happening in the aftermath of my illnesses as well as trying to maintain a happy and healthy family life. So, it stayed on the back burner.

In 2017, yet another health event presented itself and this one was to provide the most powerful motivation yet to get on with writing this book.

I woke to find that every straight line I could see had a kink in it, in fact, several kinks. Door frames, the television, pencils, buildings: everything that should have been straight was out of alignment. It was the frightening onset of a condition called age-related macular degeneration (AMD) which is a progressive disease affecting the central vision, the part of the eye used for reading or watching TV and of course, writing. I have the condition in both eyes and although there is currently no cure, the treatment I am receiving has thankfully stabilised my vision, at least for the time being. So, the writing of my book was now going to be something of a race against time as I had no idea if and when my sight would deteriorate or how rapidly.

With the help of visual aids attached to my laptop, I began the writing process and it was then I discovered how challenging this was going to be. I wrote, altered, re-wrote then scrapped all of the first chapter. Same with the second. But after persevering for a number of weeks, the project did begin to take some sort of shape. Mark Twain never made a truer observation:

Writing is easy. All you have to do is cross out the wrong words.'

But then the world changed. Struck by the horror of Covid 19 and being one of the 'clinically extremely vulnerable' group, the ensuing lockdown for me – and my wife of course – was immediate and sustained. As with many, the sudden change to our freedom and lives was devastating and adjustment was slow and tough.

However, with the unexpected amount of spare time available, I was able to concentrate almost exclusively on the writing of the book and I do wonder if there had been no pandemic, just how long it would have taken me to finish: in truth, it is likely to have remained a permanently incomplete Word document on the laptop! But it turned out to be a splendid coincidence that the book was completed in 2021, the very year of our fiftieth wedding anniversary.

I also wanted to take the opportunity of contributing something towards the search for a cure for cancer, which has claimed the lives of so many of my friends and family and continues to kill between 400 and 500 people every single day in the UK, a statistic of which I was very nearly a part. So, I am pleased to say that any proceeds from the sale of this book will go to cancer research.

My own survival is much to do with the love and unending support of my wife Lynda and our two children, Mark and Julie. That support, together with the timely intervention of the NHS, still the finest health care system in the world, has been my saviour in every sense of the word.

I hope you enjoy the book. And thank you.

"

The greatest pleasure in life is doing what people say you cannot do

"

Walter Bagehot

Chapter 1

A Dream

The Careers Officer, Miss Harrington, was a rather large, stern lady whose normal occupation was a history teacher, although there was a rather unkind rumour that in her spare time she was a lumberjack. We sat opposite each other in a corner of the classroom set aside as a temporary 'careers office' and the reason I was feeling so excited was this was going to be my first step in finding out how to become a policeman. Casting a disparaging eye over my school reports, Miss Harrington took ages before she spoke. "Well, looking at your reports," she said eventually, "your English is good and I think a job in the printing trade would suit you down to the ground."

What on earth was she talking about? I could think of nothing worse than working in a factory environment, particularly at a job I didn't want to do.

"Thanks, Miss," I said politely, "but ever since I can remember, I've wanted to be a policeman."

She stared at me as if I'd disembowelled someone in front of her.

"Goodness me, no, that's not the career for you," she said dismissively. "I'd put that out of your head straight away."

I was devastated. I had hoped for at least some encouragement from the one person, as far as I was concerned, who could point me in the right direction. "But why, Miss?" I blurted out. I felt like crying but I certainly wasn't going to let her see how upset I was.

"You don't have the necessary qualifications," she said, "and anyway, you're certainly not the right type to be a policeman."

When someone in authority puts an adverse notion such as 'you're not the right type' into the mind of a fifteen-year-old, it can have a significant long-term effect which is difficult to deal with. Miss Harrington's comment did little to boost my already lamentable lack of self- confidence and it would be some years before it improved. Nowadays, I remind myself of a brilliant quote by Eleanor Roosevelt: *'No one can make you feel inferior without your consent'* Wish I'd been able to take that on board all those years ago.

The missing qualifications Miss Harrington had referred to were General Certificates of Education (GCEs) and although I did have a School Leaving Certificate showing Passes with Credit for English General, English Essay and English Language, they were insufficient for the police service and I would need to pass a written entrance examination. Even so, I had hoped for some guidance and perhaps a little optimism from Miss Harrington. But maybe she was right: I simply wasn't good enough and as she intimated, not the right type. I didn't want to put heart and soul into trying for something that was never going to happen; but how would I ever know for sure unless I tried?

It's fair to say I didn't enjoy school much, although I did have a lot of friends which made it just about bearable. I wasn't exactly bullied but I seemed to spend a lot of time on the receiving end of verbal abuse as well as trying to dodge the occasional missile. And that was just the teachers. At junior school, the staff were content with lobbing the odd piece of chalk at us but later on they graduated to wooden blackboard rubbers as well as books and their aim often approached Olympian standard.

This was the 'baby boomer' generation with classrooms of over thirty pupils, so I guess it was sometimes a job to keep control of us all, but even so, corporal punishment did seem to be something of an art form at the schools I went to and whilst girls usually got away with a rap across the knuckles by a ruler, boys always got the cane. My first experience of such retribution was for using an 'offensive weapon' to attack a teacher; we wore short trousers with long grey socks held up by elastic garters which made superb catapults, and in the playground it was a popular sport to 'ping' each other with rolled up hardened paper pellets. We were re-enacting the battle of the Alamo or something similar when I discharged a large pellet at Davy Crockett, missed him and hit our geography teacher, Mrs Arkwright, in the ear. She was cycling through the playground when she was 'ambushed', as she put it.

The headmaster was the only member of staff who did the caning, so I was wheeled into his office and got three lashes over the fingers. My best friend Fred was less fortunate – his 'crime' was to line up twice in the dinner queue and get two semolina puddings instead of just the one we were allowed – he got six lashes when he should have been given a medal for eating two of those disgusting puddings.

I'm quite sure if the school had been allowed firing squads, they would have reduced the classroom sizes by a third in a single term. I had the cane a couple more times during my school 'career', but it really didn't leave me bitter or with a lifelong chip on my shoulder about school punishments; the thinking simply was that the rules were there and if you broke them (even accidentally) then you got punished. Apart from English, drama and some sports, the whole school education thing just wasn't my forte and I couldn't wait to leave it all behind, hence my eagerness during the final term for a consultation with our Careers Officer.

Growing up in the fifties in a village called Bingham in Nottinghamshire, the real catalyst for my aspirations to join the police was actually a television show I saw at a friend's house. We didn't have a TV at home but Gordon's parents were well off and I clearly recall standing on a thick pile green carpet in their huge drawing room and gazing in awe at the smart wood-veneered TV set which even had a wireless built into its base. There I watched my very first television programme in glorious black and white: *Dixon of Dock Green.* That show was not only responsible for the beginning of my lifelong affection for television but also for kick-starting my thinking about what I wanted to do with my life. At just ten years old, I was so impressed by PC George Dixon, this uniformed man of authority who commanded respect wherever he went, that the seed was sown. I went to Gordon's house as often as I could get myself invited so I was able to watch as much TV as possible and I became fascinated by the detective programmes of the time, *Fabian of the Yard*, *No Hiding Place* and *Interpol Calling*.

Saturday mornings were usually taken up going with my mates to the village hall to watch *Bomba, the Jungle Boy* or the latest Johnny Mack Brown western; they were often accompanied by a series of short true crime films called *Scotland Yard* as a supporting feature introduced by criminologist Edgar Lustgarten. The detectives in those films had an air of mystery about them with their trench coats and trilby hats, and I imagined what it would be like to investigate crimes and find clues that would lead to bringing criminals to justice. I really wanted to be a policeman; but most of all, a detective.

My parents were very supportive of me wanting to join the police, although it's fair to say they were a little apprehensive about my chances of success in view of my failure to pass the perceived all important eleven-plus examination and not being able to go on to grammar school. But as my mum used to say, "With hard work, it's possible to be whatever you want to be."

My parents were married on 14th August 1939, just three weeks before Britain declared war on Germany. My father was a bus driver and my mother a conductress for the same company, but on 4th April 1940 Dad was conscripted into the army, serving with the Royal Army Service Corps (RASC) as an ambulance driver. Following training, he was posted to Egypt and Mum didn't see him again for six years. He was part of the North African campaign, driving injured service men across the Western Desert, frequently under fire from Luftwaffe dive bombers as well as seeing action at the siege of Tobruk. When he was demobbed and returned home in early 1946, he was not a well man. I discovered years afterwards that he had twice been hospitalised during his war service and to this day, the reason is not known. I have acquired his entire war service record from the Ministry of Defence (MOD), including details of the hospitals, but the MOD will not disclose medical history, even to me, his next of kin.

My mother saw a huge difference in Dad's demeanour when he returned from the war; he was no longer outgoing, but became introverted and suffered frequent bouts of depression and recurring nightmares. Mum said he was 'shell-shocked,' now of course properly known as Post Traumatic Stress Disorder (PTSD) but, as with many of his comrades, it was never formally diagnosed.

On 4th December 1946, I arrived in a world struggling to put itself back together in the aftermath of WW2, and as if my parents hadn't enough to deal with, I was born with a cleft palate. Today, such abnormalities can be detected during pregnancy with an ultrasound scan, but in my case, it wasn't discovered until some months after my birth. But the delay in diagnosis proved fortunate because the National Health Service was born eighteen months after I was, in July 1948. With the resultant free treatment, Mum and Dad were able to take me to Sheffield Royal Infirmary, where I received costly restorative plastic surgery to the roof of my mouth. The cleft palate was permanently repaired, and my very first memory at three years of age is standing in a room with my parents and a smiling doctor with black, thick-rimmed glasses and a large nose who presented me with a huge sweet to suck!

For many years, Dad rarely spoke of his wartime experiences and then only sparingly, with little detail. I'm afraid to say that what he went through had little impact on me growing up; indeed, as a schoolboy I was under the ridiculous impression that everyone's father went off for the duration of the war to fight Hitler, then came home afterwards and carried on with life where they left off. It wasn't really talked about at school or when I was playing with my friends; the subject of what our fathers did or didn't do in the war just didn't arise. To my shame, the significance of what had happened to Dad only began to dawn when I reached my teens. It was then I realised that a number of men had avoided conscription, some were declared medically unfit whilst those in key industries such as engineering, farming and medicine were exempt. When I did venture to ask my mates about their fathers' war service, I was astounded to discover that within my circle of friends, Dad was in a minority. It was then I also learned what a 'conscientious objector' was. I was at Toot Hill Secondary Modern School in Bingham and around fourteen years old; one day, a group of us were lying around on the school playing field talking about WW2 when the question of our fathers' involvement came up. My best friend at the time, Ray, proudly said, "My dad was an aircraft fitter in the RAF, he went all over the world in the war."

Eric said: "My dad stayed working at the Raleigh factory."

Me: "Mine was in the army, he drove wounded soldiers in the ambulance convoys."

That was about the extent of my knowledge and I didn't really feel any particular pride in talking about Dad's war service. I damn well should have done.

Next to speak was Neil:

"My dad said war's wrong, and he just told them he wasn't going to kill a man even if he was a German."

"So did he have to go?" I asked.

"No," said Neil, proud of his father's stance. "He went to court and told them what he thought, and he won."

"So he's a Conshie!" Ray said.

I'd heard the term before but didn't know what it meant. Now I understood. Contrary to what I'd believed, not every kid's father went to war, and although I had several discussions with Dad about his experiences, I never thought to make a proper record of what he told me, which I regret to this day. But he did slowly recover from the psychological scars over the following decades, and in fact went on to join the Air Ministry Constabulary (AMC) as a MOD police officer at nearby RAF Langar.

On the school playing field, the chat turned to our future plans, and Ray was quick to announce his intention of becoming a professional footballer! Eric wasn't sure what he wanted to do but thought it would be something to do with animals whilst Neil had no doubt he was going to be a train driver. When I announced my intention of joining the police it got a mixed reception. Ray grinned and thought it quite amusing, Eric pulled a face and Neil said, "You must be joking, why the rozzers?"

"Just something I want to do," I said.

"You won't get in," Neil declared, "and anyway why would you want to join the other side?"

"I'm more interested in plain clothes work," I said, "and how do you know I won't get in?"

"Can't see that lot wanting a skinny sod like you," he sneered.

Neil's views on the police were typical of a number of schoolmates. Many of them had parents or siblings who were frequently, shall we say, at odds with the law of the land. For that reason, I rarely spoke of my ambition unless the subject arose because, apart from my parents, support for my proposed career aspirations was thin on the ground.

Just before leaving school, ignoring everyone's views as well as Miss Harrington's advice, I composed a letter to Nottingham City Police for information on the application process for their Police Cadet Entrance Scheme. On reading through the application form, I was dismayed to learn that the height requirement for male officers was 6 feet, making me ineligible by 2 inches! Despite a suggestion that I stand in a bucket of compost for three years, by no stretch of the imagination could I have made the height requirement. But Nottingham's stipulation did not apply to all forces, so my plan was to gain local employment until such time that I could leave the parental home and go to a county with smaller policemen where I could apply again.

Despite my determination to join the police, I was a shy youngster and it was a long time before I was able to shake off the nagging doubt, compounded by some of my friends and Miss Harrington, that I wasn't good enough. Or if I did get in, that I wouldn't be very effective in the job. Another of Mum's sayings was "You never know what you can do till you try." So I had a real conflict of emotions going on, resulting in a lot of confused thinking.

Something else neither my parents nor myself had properly considered, and which could create a major hurdle to my ambition, was a medical issue. When I was eleven, I developed an unusually heavy cold which left me with a series of cold sores around the mouth. They advanced into something called ocular herpes, a severe viral infection which caused an ulcer to form on the cornea of my left eye. The virus remains for life and is incurable. It stays dormant within the facial nerves beneath the skin, without any obvious problems, potentially for years, but certain stressors can reactivate the ulcer at any time resulting in a great deal of pain, and immediate treatment is needed. The stressors include trauma, excessive exposure to sunlight or severe emotional upset. Today, flare ups are treated with an antiviral medication called aciclovir, an oral tablet which, certainly in my case, is very effective. But when my ulcer first appeared in 1958, although the pain was considerable, the hospital treatment was worse.

Lying flat on my back under a huge bright light, the smell of antiseptic was overpowering and a nurse was holding my head rigidly still. A plastic covering was placed over my face with a small hole over the left eye and my eyelids pinned open with small stents so I couldn't blink. The overhead light was really intense, I could feel my eye watering and everything going blurry. The doctor said, "Ready?" In my mind I was shrieking, "No…!!!" A small stopper hovered over my left eye for a second, then a single drop left the dispenser as if in slow motion before it exploded onto my eyeball. The neat iodine felt as if a burning needle had been plunged into the centre of the eye, my head rocked violently to the side and I screamed in agony. The doctor told me to try and calm down as I squirmed out of the nurse's grip, but the pain was of a ferocity I'd never experienced and having no memory of the following two or three minutes, I must have passed out.

The procedure was carried out without a local anaesthetic and I didn't realise then, but the whole thing was something I would have to get used to; the iodine cauterisation method was to remain the standard treatment for corneal ulcers for many more years until aciclovir was discovered and eventually, thank God, approved for medical use in 1981. The real issue for me in those early years was that each time the cauterisation process took place, the resultant scarring caused a percentage of vision in the eye to be lost and my parents were warned that I should expect more episodes accompanied of course by the risk of eventual blindness in that eye.

The trauma and resultant time lost at school inevitably contributed to failing the eleven-plus examination and I just hoped that this medical issue wouldn't add to my chances of failing to have a police career. No such thing as a one-eyed copper.

On leaving school I got a job as a packer at a wholesale tobacconist in Nottingham, where I remained for the next three years, saving as much of my wage as I could. Then a real stroke of luck came my way: Dad was posted to RAF Henlow in Bedfordshire, where the local police force had a height requirement of only 5 feet 8 inches. My application letter to join the Bedfordshire Constabulary, together with my school leaving qualifications, such as they were, were in the post within a week. Would I even get a reply?

One morning six weeks later, in our new home in Clifton, Bedfordshire, I nervously tore open a letter postmarked 'Bedford' and read the typewritten contents:

'Dear Sir

I am pleased to inform you that arrangements have been made for you to attend Bedfordshire Constabulary Headquarters, Goldington Road, Bedford on Monday, 2nd August 1965 at 10 am for the purpose of sitting the entrance examination for consideration of entry to the Constabulary as a Police Constable.

Please telephone the number above as soon as possible to confirm your attendance.

Yours faithfully

Secretary to the Chief Constable'

I excitedly read the letter over and over again, I couldn't believe that at last I had the opportunity to take a first real step towards the career I wanted. All I have to do, I thought to myself, is pass this exam and then, notwithstanding my eye problem, get through a medical. 'All I have to do', dear God, it sounded so simple. All the old misgivings returned as the day got nearer and I couldn't dispel Miss Harrington's comments from my mind, try as I might. But regardless, I was going to give this my best shot.

The Pines, in Goldington Road, Bedford, was a large, austere house and the home of the county's Police Headquarters; I felt extremely jittery as I found myself ushered into a small classroom in the training department at the back of the building, where I was to sit the exam. Everything after turning over the first paper is something of a haze and I have only three clear memories of the day: wrestling with the mathematical questions, wondering what Australian sheep farming had to do with law enforcement and hearing the Rolling Stones rendition of, ironically, 'It's All Over Now' at full blast on someone's transistor radio during the bus trip home. I knew I had done the best I could but whether it was going to be sufficient, well, I would just have to wait.

Although still living at home, I needed to earn my keep, so when we moved from Nottinghamshire to Clifton, getting a job, any sort of job, was a priority. Luckily, I managed to find myself work at a Co-op supplies warehouse in nearby Hitchin. I made some good friends there but the work was as stimulating as a paving slab. If it hadn't been for the tannoy system playing non-stop music broadcast from the pirate radio station, Radio Caroline, it would have been purgatory.

Sometime after my trip to Police Headquarters, I arrived home one evening from work and Mum handed me the now familiar looking envelope.

"Good luck," she smiled, as I opened it.

I only had to read the opening words.

Dear Sir,
  I regret to inform you…

Mum knew by my face. "So sorry John," she said. "I know what it meant to you."

"I knew I hadn't done brilliantly," I said, trying to hide my crushing disappointment, "but I did think it might just have been enough."

That was it then, no police career. I should have listened, what a waste of time, effort and worry. Indeed, it was not only my qualifications that were insufficient, my general education was clearly lacking too. I would have to re-evaluate my life and think about another direction. In the meantime, at least I had a source of income at the Co-op whilst I regrouped to consider what my long-term future might be.

It was a seventeen-mile round trip to the Co-op from home in Clifton and a bit too far to cycle in all weathers, so with Dad's help I bought a used 49cc Raleigh Runabout moped, which, to begin with, was absolutely brilliant – it got me to work in twenty minutes instead of over an hour on my bike. But it was second hand with a doubtful history and an engine rattle that wouldn't go away. On two occasions, the moped almost cost me my job by breaking down on the A600 on the way in to work and with my wages increasingly used for moped repairs, I got rid of it and reverted back to pedal power. I really needed to get another job as soon as I could.

Dad established that the MOD had mounted a recruitment drive within his force, the AMC, now renamed the Air Force Department Constabulary (AFDC) and, following a lot of soul searching and discussion, I made the decision to apply for entry. At least, if successful, I would be a police officer of sorts and as Dad pointed out, there were opportunities to be had including, I was pleased to hear, the existence of a Constabulary Investigation Branch (CIB), a plain clothes crime enquiry unit based at larger RAF stations. Providing I could pass the exam and get through the medical, perhaps my future wouldn't be so bad after all, though I did wonder where it would leave me if I failed to get in. I was at a crossroads and one way or another, this was perhaps going to decide my future. As far as a law enforcement career was concerned, it was probably going to be my last roll of the dice.

With much trepidation, for the second time in six months, I sat a police entrance exam. To my immense relief, I found the exam easier than the previous one at Bedford, the usual subjects of maths, English and geography were not quite so difficult and I felt a great deal more confident afterwards. Sure enough, three weeks later, I was delighted to receive a letter from the MOD declaring that I had passed the written examination and pending a successful medical and fitness test, I would be offered a place on the force's six-week training programme. Arrangements were made for my attendance at a MOD medical centre and training ground for the second part of the application process and my world became even happier when told I had passed the medical with flying colours, including the eye test! I knew the vision in my left eye had slightly deteriorated owing to the iodine treatment, but the virus, so far, thankfully remained dormant. The fitness test proved to be something of a formality as long as I could walk, talk, breathe and run a hundred yards!

At long last I was going to be a police officer.

Chapter 2

A Toe in the Water

My six weeks at the AFDC Training School at RAF Debden in Essex was spent learning basic criminal law and police powers of arrest as well as military drill procedures, the latter deemed necessary in any uniformed body of men as a form of discipline. It was to stand me in good stead. At the conclusion of training, I was posted to No. 4 MT Squadron, RAF Kidbrooke near Greenwich in south-east London. Although the uniform and powers of arrest of my new job were the same as those of the regular police force, the job was not. It mainly entailed the manning of entry barriers at the base and various security control points within the RAF complex. Nights consisted of frequent foot patrols around the unit and making sure all sensitive buildings were secure.

It was December 1965, and I found it quite a shock to the system, as the newbie, to find myself on twelve-hour nights from 7 pm to 7 am on Christmas Eve as well as Christmas night. It didn't help that this was my first time away from home for the festive period. Over the following years, working through Christmas was often the norm and something everyone got used to, but I always remember this particular one because I hadn't had time to make many friends or acquaintances and those I had went home for the holiday, so it was a pretty boring two days in the RAF barracks with just a few airmen I hardly ever saw. My main company was Eric, a mouse that wandered into my room from behind the skirting board whenever he felt the need for some interaction or if he was feeling peckish. Conversation was a bit one-sided, but company is company.

Despite the disappointment over time off at Christmas, I certainly wasn't complaining about my lot. Compared to previous jobs, the pay was excellent at £1,300 per year, the overtime plentiful and I was proud to be Constable 366 of the Air Force Department Constabulary. A crystal clear memory of that time was on 30th July 1966 when England beat West Germany in the World Cup Final. Watching a really old black and white TV set with a wire loop aerial balanced on the top, I remember the incredible euphoria when the final whistle went after extra time signalling England's 4-2 victory. The huge crowd of airmen in the Corporals' Mess went wild; they were stood on the bar counter, tables, chairs and even the jukebox, which actually collapsed and smashed onto the floor under the sheer weight of excited, drunken humanity pressing against it. It was a disgraceful, crazy and exhilarating scene that I'll never forget.

Six months later, I was eligible to request a posting to RAF Henlow, not because Dad was stationed there but because I was hacked off with single men's quarters and my parents lived only a twenty-minute bike ride from Henlow so I could get home comforts plus save having to pay out for accommodation. The cunning plan worked, my application was granted and off I went to RAF Henlow, then the home of the Officer Cadet Training Unit and also part of the RAF College at Cranwell. I lived at home in Clifton with my parents and it was good to be back on familiar territory and see some old mates again.

Owing to the then perceived threat to UK military establishments from the Irish Republican Army (IRA), there was a policy of firearms training for AFDC officers. The training was very ad hoc – twice a year we spent a day at the firing range and half a day in a classroom. I went along on my first day of instruction with some trepidation, I wasn't particularly into guns and this would be the first time I'd held anything like a firearm since a traumatic incident when I was thirteen. I'd been messing about in Gordon's huge back garden – the Gordon of rich parents fame – playing with his air rifle, and we were firing pellets at a tin can hanging from one of the trees in their orchard (they really were rich) when one of my shots missed the can but struck down a passing sparrow mid-flight. The poor thing was killed outright and I'll never forget looking down at the little body lying in the grass and knowing I was responsible for taking its life. Gordon seemed to think it was some sort of achievement and took great delight in telling our friends about us 'hunting birds'. I hid my feelings but in truth I was mortified. Absurd as it seems now, I cried myself to sleep that night because it was down to me that somewhere a family of sparrows were without a parent or a sibling. I drifted away from Gordon shortly afterwards and often wondered what happened to him; judging by his reaction to the sparrow incident, he probably became a big-game hunter.

So here I was, seven years on, loading a Smith and Wesson .38 revolver with live ammunition and preparing to shoot at cardboard soldiers in camouflage gear. An image of the defunct sparrow flashed through my mind as I squeezed the trigger for the first time but I managed to concentrate on what I was doing and as the day progressed, I actually did quite well in terms of score. The others on the training day with me were twenty to thirty years my senior and without wishing to be too critical, if they were between me and an armed IRA man in a balaclava, I wouldn't give much for my chances. Not their fault, I think the training was more of a token approach to tick the appropriate MOD 'Officers firearms trained' box. Guns were never drawn from the armoury during my time with the AFDC, thank goodness, and I did my best to stay away from them for the rest of my service.

One day I came across an item in a Force Notices bulletin requesting applications for a month-long secondment to the Constabulary Investigation Branch (CIB) at No. 25 Maintenance Unit, RAF Hartlebury in Worcestershire. Right, this was my chance! Just what I'd been waiting for, and I immediately applied for the role. I have no idea if I was the only applicant but I was quite quickly accepted, and three weeks later found myself posted to Hartlebury. This was going to be my first taste of some proper crime investigation work. Not sure what I expected, but I thought there would probably be an office with a small contingent of detectives and plenty of minor crime to investigate.

On arrival I was instructed to report to the Detective Inspector (DI) in the police office, so on presenting myself in my new charcoal grey single-breasted suit, an off-the-peg Burton's special, I was ushered into his presence. The CIB office turned out to be two chairs with wooden arms in the corner of the main office, one of which was occupied with some difficulty by the DI, arguably the most obese policeman I'd ever seen.

"You must be Dee?" he boomed.

"Yes, sir."

"Welcome to the CIB."

"Thank you, sir." We shook hands and he said, "First things first, kettle's over there, four sugars please."

I obediently made the tea and we spent the next hour talking about the weather, football, women and in fact everything under the sun, except crime or police work. In the end I ventured, "Excuse me sir, what is the CIB strength here?"

He looked at me as if I'd grown two heads.

"You are," he said, "Norman's off sick for a few weeks so it's down to you and me."

This was more than the deep end, this was being chucked from a cliff top. With less than two years' service and no investigative training or experience, here I was answering to an officer two ranks above me and tasked with investigating crime. No pressure then. But I needn't have worried. The first week passed relatively quickly owing to the novelty of being an on-duty police officer in civilian clothes, learning about the base itself and how the RAF service police interacted with the CIB. To be honest, there wasn't a great deal to be learned after that. All I did for the remainder of my secondment was shadow the DI when he investigated various incidents involving civilian employees on the base. The 'cases' consisted of a minor assault resulting from a fight between two stewards in the NAAFI canteen, the daubing of obscene comments on the wall of a hangar and a petty larceny. This was prior to the introduction of the 1968 Theft Act and all offences of dishonesty were governed by the Larceny Act of 1916. The 'larceny' in this case related to an allegation by a mess chef that his gold fountain pen had been stolen, which turned out to be a practical joke by a member of the kitchen staff. Edgar Lustgarten would have wet himself.

The biggest crime 'we' dealt with resulted from the routine stop search of a storeman at one of the gates by our uniformed colleagues. In the employee's bag were found two electric plugs bearing the MOD arrow mark, an open and shut case of stealing government property. This was the most prevalent offence committed across most RAF stations and although we had our powers of arrest there was no point in using them as we had no cells or detention rooms in which to hold a prisoner pending the arrival of the regular police. Having no facilities or authority to charge anyone, we were duty bound to involve the local constabulary for the criminal justice system to take its course. And so it was with our storeman at Hartlebury. Despite my request to have a go, the DI took a written statement under caution from him in which he admitted the offence. A police patrol car arrived an hour later and off went the DI and the prisoner to Biggleswade Police Station to be processed. The job turned out to be a good one; when police searched the storeman's home they found a small treasure trove of electrical items stolen from the base over a period of several months. But for myself, to this day, I'm not sure why I was there, I did virtually nothing of value nor did I benefit much from the experience, apart from no shifts with a month of civilised nine-to-fives.

Back in uniform at RAF Henlow, another detachment opportunity arose, this time for twelve weeks at Headquarters Fighter Command, RAF Bentley Priory, near Stanmore in Middlesex. For the hell of it I applied and, again, got the posting. I was beginning to think nobody else ever applied for these detachments, but in this case, it turned out to be an intriguing experience.

It was 1967 and two years prior to the release of the acclaimed WW2 film, *The Battle of Britain* which was partly filmed at Bentley Priory. In 1940, the air battle strategy was conducted from the station's underground Air Defence Operations Centre (ADOC) which, to my surprise, was still in operation as a secure office environment in 1967 and our security responsibilities included control of personnel into the Centre, both service and civilian. The Centre had been the air planning headquarters for D-Day and it was a humbling experience to realise that on the day itself, the landings were monitored in this very underground bunker by King George VI, Winston Churchill and General Dwight D. Eisenhower, all of whom had passed through the little turnstile control point of which I was now in charge!

Air Chief Marshal Dowding was of course the Air Officer Commanding RAF Fighter Command in 1940 and his office in the main building had been left as it was during the war, complete with original furniture. Part of our patrol duties was to ensure the security of the building and Dowding's office in particular. In fact, the office was used in its original state in the film with Laurence Olivier playing the part of Dowding. In 2013, the Priory House was turned into a museum commemorating the role it played in the Battle of Britain and it's on my bucket list to go back and indulge in a spot of nostalgia. I thoroughly enjoyed my three-month attachment there and regretted having to leave.

Back at the sharp end, I found myself on a week of nights at Henlow. It was a Saturday evening in January 1968, snow lay on the ground, a very cold night indeed. Often only one of us was on night duty and we were expected to do a complete patrol of the camp every two hours. In those days we were not equipped with radio communications, so our safety relied upon a pre-patrol telephone call to the RAF Guardroom situated in a different part of the unit. It was 2 am and I was about to start my second night patrol when the RAF Orderly Sergeant rang me from the guardroom. In the past few minutes a man riding a stolen motorcycle had abandoned it on the edge of the camp on the boundary with the A600 road and was seen to run into the camp grounds. The civil police from Biggleswade were on their way. I headed to the general vicinity of the incident and began to search the outbuildings on the edge of the base. I struck lucky and found a set of fresh footprints in the snow leading from a gap in the almost non-existent perimeter fencing.

I certainly didn't need a sniffer dog to follow the tracks which went clearly through the camp for half a mile or so before disappearing onto the A659 Hitchin Road. About a hundred yards ahead I saw the outline of a male limping along the footpath. I shouted, "Police! Stop where you are!" He looked round then began to run, but was so exhausted that I easily caught up with him. The seventeen-year-old motorcycle thief was wet through and shaking with the cold. I arrested him and escorted him to the RAF guardroom where the local police were called. On being searched, he was found to be in possession of quite a large quantity of cigarettes and some cash which he admitted were part of the proceeds of a burglary at a local shop the previous day.

But the real learning point for me from this first arrest was to search a prisoner immediately upon detention, not only to recover any stolen property but to ensure he wasn't carrying a weapon with which to injure himself or others. The guy had a 6-inch stiletto knife in the inside pocket of his windcheater; when asked to account for it, he shrugged. I had made a serious error and one that, in different circumstances, could have ended quite differently. At Biggleswade Magistrates Court he was sentenced to three months in a detention centre for a number of offences including burglary and possessing an offensive weapon. It would be nice to think he gained as much as I did from the experience, but somehow I doubt it.

This was the time in the late sixties when the concept of Unit Beat Policing was being rolled out across all forces, where constables were permanently allocated their own local beat, several of these areas being supported by a Unit Beat vehicle, colloquially known as a Panda car. Several of the local constabulary from the Biggleswade division would call in to see us whilst on area patrol, and very welcome they were too, particularly if we were alone on a long and tedious night shift. Their stories and experiences of 'the job' were fascinating, especially when I drew parallels with my own circumstances. Having had a taste of 'real' police work with the recent arrest, my thoughts began to turn to the possibility of whether I could apply one more time to join the Bedfordshire Force because, as I had to admit to myself, boredom was beginning to set in. Without being unkind, the average age of my colleagues in the AFDC was about forty-five as opposed to my twenty-one years, and most of our duty time was spent checking in vehicles or personnel and then lifting a barrier arm. Apart from the one arrest, my police powers had remained dormant since I joined. In fact, I wasn't aware of a single arrest by a member of the AFDC, anywhere. I came to the conclusion that either we weren't doing our job properly or we were simply quite well-paid security guards! When I mentioned this to Dad he smiled and told me that after serving in the army in North Africa for the entirety of the war, he was more than happy with his lot. But he took my point and said he thought I should consider trying again to join the regular force.

It was now well over two years since my knock-back and although, at least for the time being, I was reasonably satisfied with my job, I craved excitement and stimulation, something to get my teeth into. But would the Bedfordshire Force even accept an application from a previously failed candidate from only two years ago? Even if they did, what could I do to increase my chances? I knew the answer to that before I even asked myself: I needed to take steps to increase my knowledge base. No easy task as any sort of learning course was financially out of the question, but I needed to do something to try to save the embarrassment of another exam failure.

If I was serious about this, there was only one realistic option: I made the momentous decision to dedicate my annual leave, days off and any other spare time over the following twelve months to a concentrated programme of self-education. I knew it would be a huge commitment requiring a great deal of discipline but I was determined to see it through. I invested in a series of textbooks on various subjects including a volume on maths self-help as well as a copy of the most useful book I ever came across: an edition of *Pears' Cyclopaedia*, a pocket-sized goldmine of facts, maps, myths and data on just about anything at all; undoubtedly the hard copy Google of its time! First published in 1897, it lasted until 2017 before succumbing to the digital age of the internet. I carried that book everywhere during my voluntary semester, even on night shifts at Henlow when tedium was causing the early hours to drag; I took every opportunity to read up on all manner of facts and figures, hoping at least some of it would stick.

Given shift work and the necessity of having at least some form of social life, it was quite difficult to sustain the appropriate level of study time over a period of months but I knew that would be the case when I started and I like to think it was my own motivation that ensured I stuck to the schedule. Contrary to comments by some of my work colleagues, it was coincidence that the local pub was closed for refurbishment!

Nine months after beginning my self-imposed study regime, I learned from my friends in the local force that Bedfordshire were experiencing a shortage of officers and were inviting applications. Although I would have preferred more time to study, I was advised this was an ideal time to apply. I had a little more life experience under my belt, including almost three years' service in a UK police force and with a bit of luck, I was also a tad more educated! Was it going to be enough?

Once again, off went my letter of application to the Bedfordshire & Luton Constabulary and I was absolutely delighted to receive my second invitation to attend Police Headquarters for the purpose of sitting the entrance examination. Concern that my original failed application of three years earlier would bar me from trying again was, thankfully, unfounded. I remained on a 'high' for some time after receiving the letter, this had always been my number one career choice and it was now within grabbing distance, I couldn't afford to blow this opportunity again, I HAD to get through this exam. As the day neared, my euphoria increasingly dissolved and self-doubt began to push itself to the forefront of my mind again. Of my last three 'important' tests, the eleven-plus, the first police exam and the AFDC entry test, I had failed two of them. For my future, let alone my self-respect, I needed more than anything to get through this one.

I stood outside Police Headquarters in Goldington Road, Bedford for the second time in my life and took a deep breath before approaching the big front door. The Pines was to remain as the force headquarters until 1978 when a new purpose-built HQ was built at Kempston on the outskirts of Bedford, and not a moment too soon, the old house really was bursting at the seams.

This was a Monday morning in February 1969, it was bucketing down with rain and the dark grey skies above the building added to its Bates Motel appearance and did absolutely nothing to calm my apprehension about what was ahead.

Inside, as before, it was a bustling, almost frenetic atmosphere of policemen and civilians going in and out of offices, up and down the ornate stairs and all with an air of controlled urgency about them. I later realised that the hub of the entire force's command system was in a large ground floor office here called the Information Room, from where live ongoing incidents were monitored and controlled.

Having reported to a man on the reception, I was taken again to the training department at the rear of the building where I joined another half a dozen recruit hopefuls. Our invigilator was a very tall, tough looking Sergeant who I sensed really did not want to be there. In fact, he didn't seem to want to be anywhere, the original Mr Grumpy.

"Right," he growled, once we were seated, "you have two hours, no talking and if you finish early, sit still till everyone has finished. Any questions? Good, let's get on with it."

No welcome, no introductions. Probably a good bloke to have in a scrap I thought, but hardly the life and soul on a night out.

There was a mathematics paper, English essay, geography and a general knowledge questionnaire. I don't remember too much about the actual questions apart from the essay subject, which was *Television in the Home*, and I wrote reams about that!

"Time up!" barked the Sergeant suddenly, "Pens down, stop writing now!"

I couldn't believe two hours had passed and hurriedly finished my final sentence. At least I tried to.

"I said STOP WRITING!" Sergeant Grumpy bellowed, looking directly at me. He was right of course, just that his parade ground manner towards a group of civilians, and me in particular, seemed a bit over the top. He got up from his chair and walked around the desks picking up our answer papers, glancing at them as he did so. I had stacked mine in a neat pile with the maths paper on top. As he picked them up, he looked at my maths paper for a few seconds then fixed me with a cold stare.

"These are just answers, why haven't you shown your workings?" he demanded. My heart sank.

"It didn't say I had to," I said.

"Well, I'd have thought it was obvious you need to show how you arrived at each answer," he snapped. "Anyway, too late now, the damage is done."

I left Police Headquarters feeling a combination of utter disappointment and anger. Anger directed primarily at myself for not thinking of showing my maths workings but also towards the Training Sergeant for his sheer lack of guidance. My mind was repeating his final words over and over: 'the damage is done'. Had I failed to come up to the mark? I really felt at a loss what to do next, maybe lifting barriers and searching storemen was my destiny, it certainly seemed like that now. I spent the next few weeks in something of a daze, trying to contemplate what my future might hold. Maybe after all, I should have given the printing trade a go? No, I dismissed that thought as soon as it came, far better off where I am, I reasoned, at least I'm in the game of law enforcement.

One morning a month later, I was at home waiting to go on the afternoon shift when the dreaded buff envelope with a Bedford postmark dropped on the doormat. Having picked it up, I spent about a minute staring at the thing before ripping it open.

Dear Sir,
   I am pleased to inform you that you have been successful in passing the entrance examination held at Bedfordshire and Luton Constabulary Headquarters...

I stared at the letter in complete disbelief. How could this be? YES!! WOW!! I'd done it. So, what do you think of that, Miss Harrington? Sergeant Grumpy? I was ecstatic; I knew other hazards lay ahead but this had been the single most crucial issue for me to overcome. Reading that letter vied for just about the happiest moment of my life to date!

Following the excitement of my exam success, my thoughts quickly turned to the force medical examination. I had passed the AFDC medical with ease but I knew the next one would be more stringent and probing. Then there was the fitness aspect, I had done a lot of cross country running at school and owing to the demise of my untrusty moped, I now cycled the six-mile round trip from home to RAF Henlow every day, but was it going to be enough? If not, then I would have to embark on a get-fit regime as soon as possible. I was very close to achieving my goal, so *whatever this takes,* I thought to myself, *whatever this damn well takes....*

The medical exam was certainly detailed. It concerned me that the plastic surgery to repair my cleft palate attracted considerable interest from the police doctor but it turned out to be simply a case of professional admiration! In fact, I was deemed to be almost A1 and 'fit to carry out the office of Constable'.

The 'almost' bit related to the vision in my left eye, which had slightly depleted owing to the corneal ulcer flare up when I was eleven, but there had been no reoccurrence and the other eye had 20/20 vision. I could hardly believe I had achieved the dream that began all those years ago watching the adventures of good old PC George Dixon. But I remain forever grateful to the Air Force Department Constabulary for an introduction to policing and three years of life experience, some of which, I am certain, contributed to my success in joining the 'regulars'. I worked a month's notice at Henlow and looked forward to a new and exciting police career.

Chapter 3

One Small Step

In May of 1969, I was sworn in as a Constable and following local training at Headquarters I completed an initial thirteen weeks of instruction at Eynsham Hall, the Number 5 District Police Training Centre near Oxford. Recruits from a number of forces in the south and east went to Eynsham including the Thames Valley Force and one such recruit was Mick from Banbury. We became good friends and on one or two of our occasional breaks from training we would travel to Banbury to socialise with Mick and his wife Mary. I was introduced to Mary's sister Lynda and my life changed forever. On 23rd October 1971, I made the best move of my life when Lynda and I were married with Mick as my best man. Our son Mark was born in 1976 and the family made complete in 1979 with the arrival of his sister, Julie. My personal life was happily complete.

I found the three months of initial police training an interesting experience, although the emphasis seemed to be on the academic as opposed to the practical. A sound knowledge of criminal law and police powers was of course essential and my previous training with the AFDC certainly helped, but I soon realised the only way to acquire practical policing skills and effectively interact with the public, was to be on the streets.

Whilst the law tuition at Eynsham was often difficult to get to grips with, some found the military style discipline, marching drill and physical training equally so. I'd had an introduction to that side of things from the AFDC training as well as living in RAF billets at Kidbrooke for a year, so the meticulous army type bed-pack creations followed by the Drill Sergeant's bellowed insults on the parade ground each morning didn't worry me too much. Although if you were unfortunate enough to regularly attract his attention because of scuffed boots or an inability to march properly, heaven help you:

"Smith, you are a w......! What are you?"

"A w....., Sergeant."

"You cannot even stand up straight, let alone march, can you Smith?"

"No, Sergeant."

"No, Sergeant," he would mimic. "If you don't stand up straight with your head high then I shall place a lump of lead behind your ear to balance you up. And do you know how I will place it behind your ear, Smith?"

"No, Sergeant." We'd wait for the obvious punch line.

"With a gun, Smith, with a f..... gun! Now stand up straight!"

A number of recruits would leave Eynsham Hall and thus their police career quite rapidly on almost every intake, often on day two, but sometimes within an hour of arrival. Not sure what they were expecting, but as one of the instructors said at the start of the course, "If you lot can't deal with the stuff we dish out here, you'll have no chance in the real world."

I found the food at Eynsham Hall up and down, but generally down, especially breakfast. They seemed to have a particularly unique way of preparing eggs, accurately described by a colleague:

"One day I had a boiled egg for breakfast and when I smashed the shell, the white dripped out from it onto the plate followed by the yoke which fell from the egg and went 'bonk' on the table." What alchemy were they using to produce something like that, we wondered. He further described the toast: "You could screw it up into a ball in your hand and it would gradually reform itself into a slice on your plate, like memory foam toast." I won't mention the sausages.

One of the things that stuck in my mind was the showing of an American film called *Mechanized Death*, consisting of real-life footage recorded by Ohio State Highway Patrol officers at the scenes of fatal road accidents. It was shown to us as part of an input on road traffic legislation to give an idea of what potentially lay ahead when we came to deal with serious road collisions. The film consisted mainly of close-up technicolour shots of mangled accident victims and was the most gory, invasive and blood-soaked horror film I'd ever seen; and despite the death and mayhem every police officer witnesses through their career, none of what I experienced seemed quite as graphic as some of the scenes in *Mechanized Death*. So perhaps, for me, the tactic worked!

One practical 'skill' I learned at Eynsham Hall was how to pull a pint and operate a till. We had Duty Squad days and one of them was to work behind the students' bar for an evening. Just my luck to be on duty in the bar on the same evening that the Training Centre Commandant came in unannounced, bringing with him a visiting Home Office official. Everyone rose quickly to their feet and the Commandant waved them all to sit down as they approached the bar. It all went quiet; the three of us were the centre of attention.

"Evening sir," I said in a barman-like manner, "What would you like?"

"A large scotch and ice for me, and…?" turning to Mr Home Office, who said, "Pint of lager and lime please."

The whisky was no problem, the ice more of an issue. The ice bucket on the bar counter was full and I didn't realise the contents had congealed into large lumps, but delving too eagerly with my plastic tongs into the depths of the bucket, I soon found out. The ice erupted into a meteoric shower of tiny pieces and the Commandant, showing surprising agility, ducked, so avoiding most of the onslaught. Mr Home Office didn't react so rapidly and caught much of the icy deluge in his face and down a very pristine white shirt. Mightily embarrassed, I can't remember exactly what the Commandant said although I think he was actually quite amused. Although he apologised to his guest, the latter most definitely did not see the funny side, which was unfortunate as worse was to come.

Having rescued some of the ice and served the boss's whisky, I selected a pint glass and pulled the lager for Mr Home Office. It's worthy of note that I had never been behind a bar nor served draught alcohol before. I half-filled the glass with lager followed by half a pint of lime juice. I gave the Commandant his change and my two important customers moved to a table near the bar and sat down. The students in the room, still sniggering over the ice incident, were in for a further treat at my expense. Mr Home Office took a gulp of his drink and promptly spat it out over his already damp shirt; the half pint of lime juice should of course have been a single measure, but nobody had told me. The distinguished visitor lurched backwards and knocked the table, dislodging a large glass ashtray which hit him on the leg on the way down. The whole sorry episode must have appeared like a 1940s movie comedy with this poor civil service chap as the stooge.

The Commandant apologised profusely to his damp, slightly bruised guest and guided him towards the door, but not before growling in my direction, "I hope to God you make a better police officer than you do a barman." I waited for retribution over the following day or two but thankfully nothing more was heard. Well, not at commandant or instructor level, but as word of the unfortunate incident spread, I received a mountain of 'feedback' from some very rude trainee policemen.

A useful outcome of the course was the acquisition of my Bronze Medallion for life saving. We had regular training sessions at a local indoor pool with our Physical Training Instructor (PTI), a 6-foot vociferous and musclebound Sergeant from the City of London. He did not suffer fools gladly, but I had occasion to be eternally grateful to him one evening at the pool. Wearing pyjamas to represent clothes dragging in water, we were practising retrieving various items from the floor of the deep end when my thigh muscle went into spasm whilst foraging about at the bottom of the pool. The sudden pain was excruciating and grabbing my leg I could feel the muscle bunched into a knot like a golf ball under the skin. Unable to power myself to the surface I floundered about, waves of panic began to surge through me and knowing I couldn't hold my breath much longer I thought I was going to drown. Suddenly I was gripped under my arms by a powerful pair of hands and before I knew it, was hauled rapidly to the surface. The PTI had spotted the trouble I was in. I lay on my stomach on the side of the pool spluttering and gasping for breath whilst he pressed down hard on my knee with one hand and massaged and squeezed the back of my thigh with the other. The pain slowly subsided.

"Cramp," said the PTI. "Even swimmers who know what they're doing get it."

It's interesting how we tend to remember where we were at the time of certain defining world events, for example, I vividly recall watching the 'Yes-No' interlude on Michael Miles' TV quiz show, *Take Your Pick* in 1963 when the words 'President Kennedy Shot!' came across the screen. Equally clearly, on 20th July 1969, I watched in awe with my new police colleagues at Eynsham Hall when Neil Armstrong announced, "That's one small step for man, one giant leap for mankind," as he walked on the moon. It is difficult to comprehend the enormity of that moment but I suspect we felt exactly the same as Commander Armstrong when we stepped out onto the street in full police uniform for the very first time. Apart from the mankind bit, of course.

My training ended and other than an unfortunate incident concerning a heavy night in a local pub and a pair of my police boots the following morning, nothing else particularly noteworthy happened to me on the training course. Except, incredibly, I passed.

I didn't think it would be the case, but I quite enjoyed my time at Eynsham and particularly got a kick out of the marching drill, especially at the end-of-course passing out parade. My parents were there, as indeed was Lynda, my future wife, and I felt immensely proud and a great sense of achievement in having completed the course; not to mention being able to march in time and keep in a comparatively straight line!

Eynsham Hall closed as a police training centre in 1981 and subsequently became a hotel. In 2019, exactly fifty years following that memorable introduction to policing, Mick, Mary, Lynda and myself visited the hotel for a weekend of nostalgia. The building and its atmosphere were the same as we remembered and the hotel had retained a number of displayed artefacts reflecting its police history, one of the most enduring being a corridor leading to what used to be one of the classrooms – a dozen or so police helmets had been carefully placed on the coat hooks along the wall. That was a real jolt to the memory cells and at the time something I found strangely moving.

Posted to Dunstable in Bedfordshire, I acquired 'digs' in Houghton Regis and clearly recall my first morning on duty. Enjoying that Neil Armstrong moment, I felt really proud as I began the walk from my lodgings to the police station on the other side of town. The feeling reminded me of the time my mum introduced me to my first pair of long trousers for school, a feeling of distinguished maturity mixed with apprehension. And with good cause.

As I walked to the police station a huge articulated lorry pulled up alongside me and the driver asked directions to the nearest access to the northbound M1.

I'd never been to Dunstable before my posting so the unfortunate lorry driver may as well have asked for directions to Peking, so my dilemma was a choice between appearing to be an idiot or a proficient police officer.

"Down to the traffic lights, do a left and keep going mate."

Over the last fifty years, I've wondered where the driver ended up and what he thought about the young constable who didn't know what he was doing. I worried about that for ages afterwards. My first shift that day didn't improve much either.

It was 8.55 am as I walked into Dunstable Police Station to report for duty.

"And where have you been?" snapped the Sergeant. It seemed the accepted procedure was to be at the station a minimum of fifteen minutes before duty time, but nobody had told me.

"Anyway, you're not much use to us for the time being," the Sergeant continued, "you can man the switchboard. Are you familiar with how they work?"

"No, Sergeant," I replied, glancing at the Medusa-like pile of equipment in the corner of the enquiry office.

"Good time to learn then, Enid's off sick."

So, following a ten-minute crash course from a bored looking Alf Ventress lookalike, I donned the headphones and took over responsibility for D Division's telecommunications system. The switchboard had little 'eyelid' flaps that activated when someone rang you; one eyelid flapping at a time was easy enough, three or four at the same time could be a problem. Within a few minutes of taking over, around ten or twelve activated. All I had just been told went from my head and for the second time that morning, the fingers of panic tightened.

The enquiry office constable was dealing with a member of the public at the counter and the Sergeant was in the Inspector's office. I had to sort this, so I plugged one of the leads into an appropriate eyelid jack, threw a toggle switch forward and announced with feigned authority, "Switchboard!"

"Where's Enid?" the Chief Superintendent bellowed down the line. "Been on this phone for God knows how long, what's going on, who are you?"

"Constable Dee, sir."

"Well, Dee, put me through to the DCI quick as you like."

"Yes, sir."

In a state of increasing panic I shoved the corresponding cord into another jack in the ridiculous hope that the extension might be the Detective Chief Inspector's. The odds of it being the right connection were around fifty to one against. By now the switchboard was a flight deck of moving eyelids, flashing lights and buzzing noises. Frantically trying to answer as many calls as I could, the switchboard was a mass of twisting red and black telephone cords, most of which were inserted where they shouldn't have been.

"Not your forte then, Dee?"

The Sergeant had returned and was observing the chaos. To my relief, he instructed the enquiry officer to take over the switchboard and despatched me to the kitchen to make tea.

The kettle had barely come to the boil when the Sergeant stormed into the kitchen to tell me he'd taken a call from the Chief Superintendent who wished to know why PC Dee had put him through to the mortuary instead of the DCI's office. I began to mutter something about not being trained as a telephonist but then caught the Sergeant's eye and his glare suggested I stop protesting. After just one day as an operational officer I considered my police career to be on borrowed time.

All probationers were placed with a tutor Constable for a couple of months in order to properly learn about being a police officer on the streets. Dennis was appointed my tutor and a real character he was too; he'd joined the job the year I was born in 1946 and knew everything a street copper needed to know. Every inch the archetypal bobby on the beat, he was a rotund chap with red, rosy cheeks and a magnificent handlebar moustache; no wonder he was the choice for the divisional Father Christmas each year. Whether he was patrolling on foot or on his bike, if it was a cold day, Dennis would shun the 'modern' Gannex police issue overcoat in favour of his old-style black cape, for which he was famous throughout the town. Every shopkeeper, market trader and local villain knew Dennis and although he wasn't a big drinker, every pub landlord did too. The number of 'tea spots' he had were legendary, he knew the families of the criminals who were serving time – and therefore when they were due for release – as well as who drank where, who was having an affair with who and any other piece of local gossip doing the rounds. If an investigation involved a Dunstable resident, a member of the criminal fraternity or even a local politician, Dennis was the go-to man.

Although he supervised me for only a few months, I learned so much from him. Point duty on a wet bank holiday weekend was an education, controlling the traffic en route to nearby Whipsnade Zoo and spending much of the day sheltering from heavy downpours in the doorway of the Rifle Volunteer pub. Dennis also supervised my first successful prosecution which involved a local government bigwig who had been attempting to procure an act of gross indecency in the town's public toilets. It was 1969, some seventeen years prior to the creation of the Crown Prosecution Service (CPS), so most police divisions had their own prosecutions department which were usually staffed by a combination of police and civilian personnel. Where a prisoner had been arrested and brought to a police station, the decision as to whether he/she would be charged, bailed, reported for process, or released without charge, invariably rested with the Station Sergeant or the senior officer on duty. Today, that decision is made by a CPS solicitor, and more often than not, they are involved in an advisory capacity at a much earlier stage of the investigation.

My gross indecency man had not been arrested, his identification followed complaints from members of the public that they had been accosted in the men's toilets at Houghton Turn, Dunstable, by an individual offering money to engage in a sexual act in one of the cubicles. One astute member of the public had discreetly followed the offender to his car and obtained the index number, which was registered to our man. We carried out covert observations at the toilets for the following fortnight to try to gain additional evidence but to no avail, the offender did not return. We had a good description of the suspect and Dennis suggested we take the bull by the horns, as it were, and make enquiries to locate and interview him. With no other evidence we had nothing to lose. The suspect lived in a large, detached house outside town and when we arrived, sure enough, there was the car on his drive. He turned out to be the head of a local council department in another county and one of the most arrogant people I've ever met.

It was wintertime, early evening and cold as well as dark. The first indication that we were on the right track was when the door opened. We were in full uniform and the man looking disdainfully at us answered the quite detailed description we had of the offender, even down to a pair of brown corduroy trousers. Before we could introduce ourselves, he stepped out into the cold and pulled the door behind him. He looked angry.

"And what do YOU want?" he demanded.

We had agreed that I would deal with the process in its entirety unless there was a problem. I said, "Mr Green?"

"Might be," he snapped. "What's all this about?"

"There's a matter we need to talk to you about, do you think we could go inside in the warm?"

"No," came the quick response. "We have friends here."

My hackles began to rise at the man's rudeness, especially when I thought of why we were there. I could feel Dennis's attention on me, wondering how I'd react. Keep nice and calm, just do your job.

"OK sir," I said, "we're investigating allegations of attempts to commit acts of gross indecency in public toilets in Dunstable and we have reason to believe you can help us."

I cautioned him that he did not need to say anything, etc. If I'd told Mr Green he had thirty seconds to live because I was going to shoot him, the expression on his face would have been the same. His jaw dropped and in a second his demeanour went from aggressive to apologetic.

"I'm sorry, I don't know what you're talking about," he said, almost in a whisper, looking at the ground.

"Mr Green," I said, "we need to put some questions to you which can either be done here at your home or back at the police station. Your choice."

He glanced back at the door for a second then seemed to regain his composure. "Right, well, I suppose you have a job to do, so I may as well come to the station, but I can't give you long. I'll get my coat."

He stepped quickly back inside the house and went to shut the door, but not before Dennis's size ten came down between the door and the frame, preventing it from closing.

"Do you mind?" said Mr Green, his hostile attitude returning. "I'm not going to run away!"

Dennis smiled and replied, "You never said a truer word, sir."

Turned out there were no friends present at Mr Green's home, just a confused Mrs Green. At the station, although the arrogance had gone, he did accept that he occasionally visited the toilets, including the day his vehicle number was taken. He did not admit committing the offences. With two witnesses willing to give evidence, I knew we had a good case, but the decision whether to prosecute rested with the divisional Chief Superintendent. It was a sensitive issue owing to who the suspect was, i.e., a high profile senior local government officer in a neighbouring county and also a leading figure in several charitable organisations within our own community.

To my mind, there was no doubt about his guilt, but presumably he had far too much to lose to admit an offence of this nature. Fortunately, the divisional commander agreed with my view and Mr Green was summonsed to appear at Dunstable Magistrates Court. Incredibly, and contrary to expectations, he pleaded guilty to a single offence of attempting to procure an act of gross indecency; with no previous convictions and following a strong plea of mitigation by his solicitor, he received a two-year probation order. My first successful case.

Chapter 4

Learning the Ropes

Dennis was one of the few remaining old-style policemen and with the introduction of the 'Panda car' Unit Beat type of policing, he knew his era was declining. Something he said once stayed with me, and I failed to realise its significance at the time. He was having an argument about the policing of a forthcoming public order event with a Superintendent in the rear yard at Dunstable Police Station. An increasingly annoyed Dennis was saying, "With the greatest respect sir, you're bloody well wrong, we're not in Russia and we can't police without having the public behind us and supporting us!" Didn't mean much to me at the time as said Superintendent stormed off with Dennis muttering, "Bloody moron." Of course, policing by consent is, and has been since the time of Robert Peel, a cornerstone of the job and Dennis understood that binding principle years before it became a government slogan. He didn't tell me what the Superintendent was proposing, but it was well known that sparks always flew between the two of them, and it was usually worth watching; despite his lower rank, Dennis was never afraid of authority.

I was out with him at all times of the day and night, and he would introduce me to so many useful contacts, but I think he knew deep down that we wouldn't be able to carry on the tradition of perpetuating such contacts simply because the style of policing was evolving rapidly, becoming much more 'motorised' and therefore less personal. A crying shame, but I feel very privileged to have experienced something of being a 'real' policeman on the beat, albeit for such a short time, before massive budget cuts and so-called progress launched the job inevitably into an advancing world of more detached high-tech law enforcement.

The first two years of police service is a probationary period in which the officer is constantly assessed and a decision made as to his/her suitability to remain. The pressure is on to make a good impression. My first few months in the job had gone well, having a few arrests, some amusing moments and calamities as well as one or two grim experiences, all of which every police officer comes across.

It was announced that our section had a new shift Inspector who was known to be a strict disciplinarian; we were instructed to pay particular attention to our uniform turnout, making sure boots were polished and trousers pressed etc.

In a nod to the time when the police service had a more military structure, we still had to 'parade' on duty at the start of every shift by standing in line and, depending on who the Duty Inspector was, produce our 'appointments', which I seem to recall were truncheon, handcuffs, whistle and pocket book. On this particular morning we lined up ready for the new boss and at 7 am precisely, into the parade room he came, a 6 foot 2 inch ex-Guardsman of ultra-smartness. The Sergeant called us to attention and the Inspector walked slowly along the line, looking us up and down without saying a word. Then he got to me. I stared straight ahead, willing him to continue along the line, which of course he didn't. He said loudly:

"Where's your whistle?"

Under normal circumstances, such a comment would have provoked a little merriment, but not this time. Glancing down, I was aghast to see that my whistle chain was not in its rightful home between buttonhole and breast pocket. For the first time ever, I had forgotten to wear the thing, and it had to be today. And it was a double whammy of dismay because I instantly recognised the Inspector's voice as that of Sergeant Grumpy. My invigilator had been promoted and sent from Headquarters to Dunstable to torment me.

"Sorry, sir," I mumbled, "I forgot it."

"So, you actually made it into the force then?" he said, sarcastically.

"Yes, sir."

"Well, you need to buck your ideas up, with this sort of sloppiness you won't make it through your probation."

Really? For a missing whistle, a piece of equipment that even in those days in the late sixties was obsolete? It seemed Mr Grumpy had taken a dislike to me from the outset, but with him being the new shift boss, I was going to have to work hard to keep him off my back.

One day soon afterwards, I was on duty in the communications room, it being my turn as the section radio operator, when I received a phone call from my opposite number at Bedford.

"Is PC Dee on duty?"

"Speaking."

"Oh, hello. Some bad news for you I'm afraid, mate. Sorry to tell you, your mother's dead."

The words didn't register for several seconds then as realisation dawned, I felt my pulse quicken and everything went distant. What was he talking about? My mum, although overweight, was reasonably fit and well; I'd spoken to her and my dad a few days earlier and had no cause for concern. There had to be a mistake.

"Are you sure? What happened?" I heard myself say.

"We don't know yet, she collapsed in the street. So sorry."

As it happened, there was nothing anyone could have done. Mum had collapsed from a fatal heart attack in a telephone kiosk. Had she felt ill and tried to call for help?

We would never know. Devastated, I took annual leave and returned home to be with Dad and help deal with the aftermath of a hundred things to be resolved following a sudden family bereavement.

I later discovered that Inspector Grumpy, let's now call him Inspector Evans, had not only unofficially converted my annual leave to compassionate leave, thereby saving me having to use up my allocation, but had also extended it by a week. Dad did not have a car at the time, and I was a non-driver so Inspector Evans also made arrangements for a police car to be put at our disposal as and when needed. I will always be grateful to the force in general but Inspector Evans in particular for the invaluable support provided over that awful period. When I thanked him for his help some time afterwards, the response was typical: "Just make sure you come to work properly dressed in future."

I thought there was the glimmer of a smile when he said it, but it was probably a trick of the light…

Lesson learned: never take anyone at face value on a first meeting.

I threw myself back into work once more but within days came a stark reminder of what the doctors had told my parents at Nottingham General Hospital a decade earlier. The virus, always lurking beneath my skin, reacted to the significant stress I had been under and for the second time, revived the corneal ulcer on my left eye.

At the Luton and Dunstable Hospital, the dreaded iodine procedure took place once more and another small percentage of damage to my eye resulted. My mind was in turmoil, I was due to take a police driving course at some point, a precursor of which was to undergo an eyesight test. The ulcer could spell the end of my police career before it had properly started. I remained off sick for a couple of weeks, dreading what was going to happen when the bandage came off. Luckily, a series of eye tests at the hospital revealed that despite scarring caused by the treatment, my vision had deteriorated only fractionally and in truth I noticed little difference to my sight. What a relief! I prayed for no further anguish or severe trauma which might reactivate the virus, severely affect my vision and potentially end my career.

On returning to work at Dunstable, my tutor Dennis was on leave, so under strict instructions not to get into trouble I was despatched to the town centre to carry out a foot patrol. As always, strolling down the high street I was feeling immensely proud to be wearing the uniform of the office of Constable. I felt quite weighed down, what with a wooden truncheon that fitted neatly into a special trouser pocket, a pair of handcuffs in a pouch on my belt and two sections of a Pye Pocketphone radio, the transmitting half of which had a pop-up aerial that went up your nose if you weren't careful when using it in a hurry. But of course, we were naked compared to the amount of equipment modern day officers have to wear, from stab proof vests, tasers and extendable batons to cuffs, mobile phones and incapacitant sprays. It amazes me they can manage to walk upright, let alone give chase to anyone.

Speaking of walking upright, there I was, proudly patrolling High Street North, Dunstable, on a rare solo outing as a fully fledged officer. As I was passing what seemed to be the longest bus queue in the world, my attention was momentarily distracted by a lady in a really short black leather mini skirt walking along the pavement past the Old Sugar Loaf Hotel on the opposite side of the road. Although only a split second, it was sufficient for me to walk at 2.5 miles an hour into a lamp post. My helmet catapulted from my head and bounced into the centre of the A5. Before I could even think about trying to recover the thing, a Mothers Pride lorry ran over it. I stared in frozen shock at what looked like a vinyl long-playing record gently quivering in the road. At that moment, if someone had handed me a loaded pistol, I swear I would have blown my brains out.

The presence of the bus queue slowly dawned; it seemed that Dunstable's entire population had come together to witness the worst thing that had ever happened to me in my short policing career. I gingerly picked up what was left of my head gear – a big black disc – from the side of the road before slinking away. It's barely possible to slink when wearing full police uniform in a busy high street, but I managed it. The inevitable comments followed me along the street:

"Put it back on your 'ead mate!"

"Stick some pedals on then you can ride it back!"

And the most cringe-worthy:

"Lecherous sod, I saw what you was looking at!"

I can only imagine what a prisoner walking to the gallows must have experienced but it couldn't have been a million miles from what I was feeling during that journey of shame back to the police station. The only time I have been in similar depths of embarrassment was on 2nd June 1953, on the occasion of the Queen's coronation when I was just six years old. Half a dozen other local children and I were in a large open back truck being pulled along by an agricultural tractor. We were dressed as soldiers with bright red tops, khaki shorts and cardboard swords as part of a carnival convoy driving slowly through the village. It seemed to me that thousands of people were lining the streets waving little paper union jack flags and cheering, but it was a small village and I guess the true number was about fifty. Halfway through the journey, I needed the toilet. Like immediately. The supervising lady on the truck was busy rendering first aid to a little boy whose ear had been poked by a cardboard sword, so I didn't say anything. It would have been too late anyway, the wet warm feeling was gently spreading over the front of my khaki shorts, clearly visible to the multitude thronging the street. With no refuge and nothing to hide my plight, I remained steadfastly at my post, cheeks the colour of my top. I don't recall the crowd's reaction but mine was sheer embarrassment as I felt the trickle running down my leg. Sixteen years on, here I was again, the truck substituted by Dunstable High Street with the same feeling of humiliation deep in my stomach.

When I told the Sergeant what had happened to the helmet, to say he was angry is like saying the *Titanic* only half sank, he was apoplectic. After calming down slightly, he said he had a good mind to drill two holes in what was left of the helmet and thread a pink ribbon through as a chin strap, then send me out down the high street again. I thought that was a bit of an unjust comment under the circumstances.

You'd think it would be impossible to reach similar depths of public humiliation yet again, wouldn't you? Soon afterwards on a bank holiday Monday, I was sent to the town centre crossroads to carry out point duty. In theory, controlling two crossing lines of traffic is relatively simple and indeed the first ten minutes went reasonably well, the problem arose when vehicles wanted to turn right and vehicles coming from the opposite direction wanted to turn left at the same time. If not carefully controlled, the centre bit when they're adjacent to each other grinds to a halt. And grind to a halt it did.

An aerial view would have resembled a shambolic mechanised cattle market with me at the centre. At ground level, horns began blaring, engines revving and drivers leaning from their windows shouting obscenities. Being utterly helpless to resolve the chaos was bad enough but knowing I'd caused it as well... I prayed again for that loaded pistol. With no convenient trapdoor in the A5, desperate measures were called for, there was only one thing for it.

A particularly aggressive Austin Cambridge was nosing towards me, so I stepped onto its front bumper bar and then onto the bonnet. God knows what the driver thought I was going to do; my intention was simply to extricate myself from this carnage in any way I could and resign from the force. I hopped from the Cambridge's bonnet to that of a polished red Cortina and bearing in mind the impact of my heavy black leather boots (now dried out from their Training Centre adventure) on his pride and joy, I guess the driver's display of naked fury was to be expected. Not only could he not turn left anymore, he couldn't go anywhere at all and to top everything, his car was being vandalised. By a policeman.

"You stupid bastard!" Mr Cortina screamed., "Look what you've done to my motor!"

Leaping onto solid ground and without a backward glance at the devastation, I walked casually back to the station to an even more uncertain future. Incredibly, Messrs Cambridge and Cortina did not make a complaint and neither did any of the other motorists. Perhaps they didn't want to take the risk of their vehicles being crushed or towed away by the police whilst they reported me... but had they made a formal complaint, it is certain these pages would not have come to be written.

I did point duty lots of times after that and I must have improved somewhat as one night we were called to a road accident on the Luton/Dunstable border which had caused a gridlock around the A505 Poynters Road crossroads junction.

It was well after midnight and whilst my colleague dealt with the two vehicles involved in the accident, I did my best to direct traffic around the scene. It was going reasonably well, albeit slowly, when I became aware of a Rolls Royce Corniche edging towards me. It drew level, its window lowered and the driver said, "Doing a good job there, young man." Praise indeed from Bruce Forsyth on his way home from an appearance at Cesar's Palace Casino and Nightclub, situated a few yards from the scene of the accident.

At the time, Cesar's was one of the premier cabaret nightspots in the country and I was to spend many pleasurable evenings there over the next decade or so. But it was nice to see Bruce. To see him, nice.

Sometime afterwards I took my dad to Cesar's. It was about a year after Mum's passing and one of his favourite artistes, Max Bygraves, was the cabaret act for the weekend. Some weeks earlier I had been introduced to George Savva, the manager of Cesar's at the time, and he kindly arranged for my dad and myself to go backstage at the end of the show to meet Max who couldn't have been more gracious. The two of them chatted for half an hour and Dad said it was one of the most memorable evenings he'd ever spent.

Cesar's regularly featured stars from both sides of the Atlantic: Shirley Bassey, Frankie Laine, Roy Orbison, Jack

Jones, Johnny Mathis, Tommy Cooper, Cliff Richard, Neil Diamond, Danny La Rue, the list was endless. Cesar's was also a handy venue for a number of artistes who lived locally; Bob Monkhouse lived at Eggington, near Dunstable, and was a frequent top of the bill at Cesar's, as indeed were the Leighton Buzzard-based Barron Knights pop group. Eric Morecambe lived at Harpenden, a twenty-minute drive from the club, and was well known for his involvement in many local initiatives including of course his position as a director on the board of Luton Town Football Club.

The American singer Billy Daniels once appeared at Cesar's for a week and unbeknown to George Savva, Billy was a particular favourite of the notorious Kray twins. One evening Ronnie and Reggie Kray arrived at the club with their entourage, having booked a table of ten. They went backstage afterwards where they drank champagne with Billy Daniels until 2 am, but the staff were more than happy as it seems the party were exceedingly generous tippers. As George said at the time, "Business is business!"

One of the inevitabilities of police work is death in all its forms and I'll always remember the circumstances surrounding seeing my first dead body outside of the family. Whilst at the Luton and Dunstable Hospital on a routine enquiry at the mortuary, the body of Reginald Stevens was brought in, the poor man having been blasted with a sawn-off shotgun at point blank range during the course of a post office robbery in Luton. The sight of the ravaged body had a huge impact on me, it was the first fatal victim of violence I'd seen and was a reminder that individuals capable of cold-blooded murder were real, were out there and had to be dealt with by us, the guardians of society.

The case attracted national interest and was investigated by Detective Chief Superintendent Ken Drury, head of Scotland Yard's Murder Squad. In March 1970 at the Old Bailey three men were subsequently convicted for the murder and sentenced to life imprisonment: Patrick Murphy, David Cooper (real name John Disher) and

Michael McMahon received a recommendation that they serve a minimum of twenty years.

Drury was subsequently promoted to Commander and became head of the Flying Squad. But he was a devious and corrupt officer, his downfall eventually coming in July 1977 when he was convicted on five counts of corruption in relation to his links with the Soho pornography trade and sentenced to eight years' imprisonment (later reduced on appeal to five).

His investigation into the Luton murder was similarly corrupt, and Murphy, Cooper and McMahon were proved innocent and only released after the influential writer and justice campaigner Sir Ludovic Kennedy's book about the case, *Wicked Beyond Belief*, was published in 1980.

Like every police officer I was of course to see a lot of dead bodies during my service and although none had quite the effect of the first one, it was something I never quite got used to, nor became comfortable with.

Another major Luton crime which had a considerable impact on Dunstable's division at the time was an armed robbery which took place in April 1970 at the National Westminster Bank in George Street, Luton where staff and customers were held up by four men armed with shotguns and revolvers. They stole £32,625 and escaped in a stolen Rover which was later seen in Houghton Regis and subsequently pursued by patrol officers. The car crashed on a sharp bend near Charlton and the offenders decamped.

Two officers, PC Brendan Walsh and PC Colin Jones, who had led the pursuit, ran after them on foot and, despite being fired at a number of times, managed to arrest one of the robbers. Firearms and £29,000 of the stolen cash were recovered from the crashed Rover. At Nottingham assizes on 24th June 1970, the man arrested was sentenced to ten years' imprisonment and both officers were commended by the Director of Public Prosecutions, the trial judge and the Chief Constable. The following year they were awarded the British Empire Medal for gallantry by Her Majesty the Queen.

Whilst awaiting a driving course, much of my time was necessarily spent working in the enquiry office and whilst most of it was mundane, there were some moments of interesting activity. Such as the middle-aged gent who came into the police station two days before Christmas and said to me, "Officer, I broke into Britain Street School last night and I want to give myself up." Before I could question him further, the Station Sergeant came from behind me, opened the counter flap and said, "Come in, Brian, you're a bit late this year." Seems Brian was what you would call an 'institutionalised burglar' with a string of convictions for breaking and entering, theft, minor fraud and just about anything else connected with dishonesty. It was a sad case, he was homeless and although making his living from thieving, many of his offences were committed in the run up to Christmas so he would be remanded in custody and spend the festive season in the comparative warmth and safety of Bedford Prison. The probation service as well as a succession of social workers had tried unsuccessfully over a number of years to rehouse and/or rehabilitate him but he seemed strangely content with his way of life. The Sergeant's comment sadly reflected the establishment view: "A pleasant enough villain, but a lost cause."

On the enquiry office main desk sat a bright red telephone used only for receiving emergency 999 calls. A number of the calls received on the 'bat-phone' made me seriously wonder about the mental state of some members of society:

"I've locked myself out."

"I heard on the radio that the motorway's closed, what time will it open?"

"I'm really late for a meeting at the town hall, is there any chance of a police escort?"

"My dog went missing an hour ago, has he been handed in to you? Just that he has a really nervous disposition."

Then there were the nuisance ones with false reports of road accidents, fires or armed robberies, all of which needed a response in case they were happening for real. One evening, there had been a spate of such nuisance calls and I was becoming increasingly annoyed. When it next rang, I grabbed the handset:

"Police emergency!"

An inebriated male voice: "My mate's refusing to buy the next round, if you don't send somebody to the Red Lion now, I'm going to murder him."

The red mist came down. "Then go ahead!" I said sharply, "and ring me back when you've done it so I know who to arrest!"

I slammed the phone down. In those days half a century ago, the emergency telephone had only a single line so if it was engaged with a false call, someone in real distress would not get through, resulting in potentially serious consequences. Within minutes, the bat-phone rang again. Was it my drunk caller again? As I lifted the receiver, I heard a great deal of shouting and screaming, it certainly sounded like a pub environment.

"Police emergency!" I shouted down the phone, in an effort to be heard. "What's the problem?"

The panic-stricken reply came as something of a shock.

"He had a gun and he's shot Charlie Pope!"

Oh my God, please don't tell me the drunk caller earlier took my advice and shot his mate for not buying a drink! Couldn't be.

"Calm down and tell me what's happened," I said, adopting the calmest voice I could summon. "Firstly, where are you?"

"The Unicorn in Luton, I think it was Graham French did it, but Charlie needs an ambulance!"

This wasn't the drunken fool from earlier, but a genuine shooting incident needing immediate police and ambulance attendance. The subsequent investigation resulted in former England youth international footballer Graham French, at the time playing for Luton Town, being convicted of attempted murder and serving a three-year prison sentence. Lesson learned: be professional, stay calm and think before you speak!

Chapter 5

Accidents and Celebs

During my first two years of service, I dealt with a number of fatalities under varying circumstances. The first was a road accident which had occurred in the early hours of the morning involving a single car in a remote lane near a village called Little Billington.

I was crewed with my Patrol Sergeant and we were the first to arrive at the scene ahead of the other emergency services. The car had struck a tree and overturned. The driver was a young man in his twenties who was partway out of the driver's side window and the car was on top of him, he'd been virtually decapitated. A pathologist confirmed he would have died instantly. There was a comparatively small amount of alcohol in his system so although the coroner's verdict was accidental death, the definitive cause of what made the driver swerve into a tree was never discovered.

There was no doubt about the cause of death of another young man who had been driving several friends at high speed along Whipsnade Road, Dunstable, following an evening of drinking. At the coroner's inquest it was estimated that he attempted to take a downhill offside bend at around 70 mph. The vehicle left the road, overturned and rolled into a ditch. The scene was a bloodbath and it was a miracle that only the driver died, his three passengers escaping with serious but non-life-threatening injuries. All were merely teenagers and when I went to the hospital to carry out initial interviews with the survivors days afterwards it was obvious that the grief and shock was going to stay with them for a very long time.

Without doubt, the worst kind of death to deal with concerns children. One summer morning I was sent to a reported cot death in one of Dunstable's outlying villages.

The parents were in a state of complete devastation and when I looked at the little boy's tiny lifeless body lying in his cot, it was all I could do to hold it together. At the time my son, Mark, was the same age.

Every sudden, violent or unexpected death has to be properly investigated and immediate processes need to be implemented which can appear harsh and unfeeling to those closest to the deceased. There had been some domestic issues involving these particular parents during which social services had become involved, resulting in the attendance at the house of the CID and a Scenes of Crime Officer (SOCO).

However, a post-mortem revealed the cause of death to be cardiac arrest due to respiratory failure but as in so many cases of what is now known as Sudden Infant Death Syndrome, the root cause of the respiratory failure remained unknown, making it even more difficult for the parents to come to terms with their loss. That evening when I arrived home, I held my baby son a little closer.

Lynda and I had married in 1971 and moved into our first home, a detached police house we were really lucky to get, in the village of Toddington. It had an office attached to the side, on the roof of which was fitted a nuclear attack early warning siren. The sirens were part of a national communications system required to warn the public of an imminent air attack or the approach of nuclear fall-out. The Cold War was at its height and regular testing of the messaging equipment and siren was deemed essential. The speaking clock provided a national ready-made system of distributing the messages along its phone lines and at a specific date and time, police stations and designated police houses were issued with a code word which was the signal to briefly test the siren.

To be constantly ready to receive messages the Carrier Control Point equipment in the office was always 'live' and so of course was the siren activation button. Many of the more remote police houses had them and I guarantee all of their occupants had a story to tell, usually involving parties, alcohol or children. I had a mischievous young nephew at the time and one Sunday afternoon the red button on the office wall became irresistible to a four-year-old finger. The rising screaming wail of the siren was deafening and must have sent many of the village's older citizens into hysteria for a second or two before they realised it wasn't an air raid. It conjured up an image of Corporal Jones from *Dad's Army* running up and down his living room shouting, "Don't panic! Don't panic!"

Despite its hiccups, the system was deemed to be secure and effective, and in fact remained in place nationally until finally decommissioned in 1992.

The 'village bobby on his bike' concept had passed into policing history a few years earlier with the advent of Unit Beat Policing and the introduction of the Panda car system. However, the public, and especially it seemed, the residents of Toddington, were somewhat unwilling to accept the change. Rural police houses, such as ours, had to retain not only the civil defence warning equipment but more significantly, the constabulary signage including an illuminated 'Police' sign over the front of the garage. So, it was no wonder everyone thought it was business as usual and that when I wasn't there, Lynda was a part of the police service who could take in lost dogs and accept vehicle document productions from irate motorists who had been caught speeding! Lynda was a teacher at the time and had acquired a post at a nearby school in the village; in fact, it couldn't have been nearer, it was next door to the police house, so everything considered, we regarded the occasional knock on the door on police business as a fair trade off!

Almost every town has its own local hero, perhaps a sports personality or someone in showbiz. Cliff Field was a born and bred Dunstable boy who began his boxing career after joining the navy at fifteen. He won his first professional fight in 1968 with a knockout in just over two minutes. His second opponent was knocked out in less than five minutes and he went on to win the next seven fights.

Known on the boxing circuit as 'Iron Man', Cliff was a popular gentle giant character who did occasional work as a doorman at the Key Club in the town and sometimes worked for his uncle Vic who owned a local car breakers yard.

In the course of his career he sparred with Brian London, Joe Bugner, George Chuvalo and was even invited to go on an exhibition tour with possibly the greatest of them all, Muhammad Ali. The tour included London, Milan and Rome with Cliff having several sparring rounds with the great man himself.

One morning I was in the police station canteen when a call came in that Cliff was in the local high street milk bar and was wanted on a failing-to-appear warrant in connection with a domestic issue. Three or four of us jumped into a police van and headed off to the milk bar being only too aware that as a successful heavyweight boxer if Cliff didn't want to come with us voluntarily, then we just might need the cavalry. Having seen us draw up outside the milk bar, Cliff legged it down the high street. We jumped out the van and ran after him with me somehow in the lead. Cliff seemed to be jogging whilst I was running as fast as my legs would carry me but he was getting further and further in front.

I thought that if I didn't do something pretty soon he was easily going to outrun us, so with a superhuman (to me) burst of energy I got a bit nearer to him then launched a rugby tackle designed to bring him down so we could all jump on him. As if in slow motion Cliff turned his head towards me just as the tackle was launched, neatly sidestepped and for the second time in my career, I hit a lamp post. My knee collided with it, the pain was excruciating and I thought I'd broken my leg. Cliff saw what had happened, stopped running and came back towards me with his arms extended in preparation for the handcuffs which were duly put on him by my colleague Ken who had been immediately behind me. I'll always remember Cliff's concern looking down at me and asking if I was OK as he was led away to the van.

It was a fairly severe knee injury which necessitated a month or so off work but with no permanent harm done.

Sometime afterwards, I bumped into Cliff in the Pheasant pub in Dunstable and he apologised for the incident. I told him it was one of those things that went with the territory. We shook hands, had a beer and that was that.

Cliff's impressive professional career was sadly cut short in 1971 when the British Boxing Board of Control revoked his licence due to concern over his ability to withstand further punishment to his left eyebrow which had been prone to splitting.

But he then enjoyed a successful series of bouts in the unlicensed fight game and on 4th December 1978 became the unofficial heavyweight UK champion having knocked out the title holder, Lenny McLean. To reinforce his right to the title, Cliff again defeated McLean in a return fight in February 1979. Over the following years, his health deteriorated and he lost an eye as a result of being glassed during a fight outside a Luton club. He sadly passed away in 2010 at the comparatively young age of 67, but he remains a legend in the town. RIP, big man.

Dunstable has hosted a number of celebrities in the past, perhaps the most well known being one Frank James Cooper, better known as cinema western hero, Gary Cooper. His father had emigrated to Montana, USA from Houghton Regis and his mother had emigrated to the US from Kent. They married and Gary was born in 1901. His mother decided she wanted him and his brother, Arthur, to receive an English education so she brought them back to the UK where the brothers were enrolled at Dunstable Grammar School. They studied there for three years, returning to live in Montana in 1912. The Gary Cooper public house in Dunstable is named in recognition of his connection to the town and the bar has an impressive statue of him on horseback.

Another ex-Grammar School pupil was the actor Sam Kydd, who was to feature in the 1960s television series, *Crane*, and the sequel, *Orlando*. The Northern Ireland and Manchester United football legend, George Best, came to play at Dunstable in 1974 and although he only played in two friendly matches, it was a huge tonic for the club and the town. A decade earlier, in January 1964, Dunstable Football Club had hosted the town's Pioneer Boys' Club against a Showbiz XI which comprised, amongst others, singers Tommy Steele, Kenny Lynch and Ronnie Carroll as well as actor Harry Fowler (Corporal 'Flogger' Hoskins in TV's *The Army Game*).

The lead singer of the popular band the Barron Knights, Richard Palmer (stage name Duke D'mond), was a Dunstable boy and in fact the rest of the group hailed from nearby Leighton Buzzard. But for two decades from 1969, the real 'in' place for much of the southeast of England was the largest and most popular music venue outside London: Dunstable's California Ballroom. It is hard to think of a music act from that era who did not play the 'Cali'. The Rolling Stones, Tom Jones, the Drifters, Dusty Springfield, Roy Castle, the list goes on. But I won't forget the night one particular group played the Cali.

One of the lessons I learned early in my career was always listen to advice from my peers, especially those older and wiser; the trouble is, when you're young and zealous it can be a difficult one to learn. One evening, an army of two were briefed by the Duty Sergeant in the parade room at Dunstable Police Station.

"Just keep an eye on things," were the Sergeant's instructions to Dennis and me, "and radio in if you need help."

If he was aware that one of the country's top rock bands was performing to a capacity crowd at the Cali, he didn't let on. The task was to make sure the punters behaved themselves when they left the nightspot. Two of us. Right.

Ninety minutes later, the main exit and fire doors of the club were flung open and hundreds of people emerged in a hurry. They were laughing, yelling, swearing. And fighting. The local press quoted 'a crowd of 1,300 jammed into the ballroom' that night but the California management stated that the capacity of the venue was 3,000 and that evening they estimated there were 3,500 in the ballroom with a further 500 in the bars and spilling into the car park.

As my mentor radioed for reinforcements he said, "We'll let the dust settle a bit lad, easier to pick up the pieces." Should have listened to Dennis of course, but the adrenaline was pumping and I thought something needed to be done to calm things down. Stupid boy.

On launching into the mass of drunken humanity, fooling myself the uniform would be some sort of respected shield, my feet went from under me and my helmet went flying yet again. As I hit the concrete on my back, there were lots of not so friendly faces staring down at me and as the kicking began, I rolled myself into the foetal position for some protection. The scale of my stupidity began to dawn and I knew that unless something happened soon, this was not going to end well. I became aware of Dennis, bless him, trying to charge his way through this ugly mob, throwing people out of the way in his efforts to reach me and at least one of my aggressors got cracked across the shoulders by Dennis's truncheon. Then came the most heavenly sound I'd ever heard in my life.

Even today, the throaty bark of a German Shepherd dog takes me straight back to that night. The kicking stopped, the crowd parted in a flash and suddenly I could see the night sky. Zimba was in full warrior mode and there were a number of thugs that night who would have to explain to parents or partners the presence of some severe teeth marks around their nether regions. Zimba and his handler, Terry, were a fearsome combination and in a public order situation were worth twenty officers. Since school days my ambition was to become a detective but that night I resolved that if for whatever reason it didn't happen, I would be a dog handler. The force had an excellent dog section and even today, there are countless examples of members of the public and police officers being saved from serious injury by these amazing partnerships.

This was 24th June 1972 and the rock group, Slade, had finished playing, the bar was closed and everyone wanted to leave at the same time. The mix of lager and frustration had led to the inevitable, but fortunately for me the troublemakers had reckoned without Bedfordshire's finest. The night van arrived, there were several arrests and the crowd rapidly dispersed. I wasn't seriously hurt, just a few scratches and some bruising with the only other casualty being my helmet which was retrieved from the car park and although not as flat as the first one, was a close second.

Lesson learned: heed advice when it's given. As Confucius once said: 'Real knowledge is to know the extent of one's ignorance.'

The DJ that night was Bruce Benson, a local 'celebrity' and self-styled entrepreneur who was active in the Dunstable area from the late sixties through to the eighties. A complex character, I met Bruce a number of times, and although it has to be said he loved being the centre of attention, he was a good DJ, resident at the California as well as having his finger in a number of other showbusiness pies. One such pie involved the setting up of Strawberry Productions, booking acts to appear at various venues around the country and his work included managing singer Kathy Kirby's comeback.

For a short time during the mid-eighties he became the manager of Eddie Kidd, the motorcycle stunt rider. Bruce knew that my young son was a particular fan of Eddie and one day told me they were having a business meeting at his home in Eaton Bray if I would like to bring Mark along to meet him. So, I piled my lad and a young friend of his into my car and ten minutes later they were chatting away to Eddie Kidd. I found Eddie a very charming man with a great deal of humility and a cracking sense of humour.

In 1996 I was shocked to read of his last jump across an airstrip near Stratford-upon-Avon. It was, to him, a comparatively simple jump of 50 feet which he completed but when the wheels hit the ground he struck his chin on the petrol tank and was knocked unconscious. Out of control, the bike plunged over a 20-foot embankment, leaving Eddie with serious head and pelvic injuries. He remained in a coma for three months leaving him paralysed and with brain damage. It was a catastrophic end to an amazing career in which Eddie had performed over 12,000 motorcycle jumps, perhaps his most memorable being as actor Harrison Ford's stunt double in the 1979 film, *Hanover Street* in Shepton Mallet, Somerset, when he jumped 120 feet over a railway cutting at a speed of 90 mph. The boys never forgot their meeting with Eddie and I will always be grateful to Bruce for arranging it.

A year after that fateful jump, Bruce Benson himself passed away. He was found in a fume filled car near a remote picnic spot in Bedfordshire. Bruce was the original lovable rogue and despite his sometime popularity, doubtless had his critics but it was sad to see such a small congregation at the funeral. Whatever his faults, Frank Sinatra's song told us as we left the church in Eaton Bray that Bruce had indeed done it his way.

I was to remain carrying out mainly foot patrol or enquiry office duties, as well as being an occasional mobile patrol co-pilot for the first four years or so of my service but then one glorious day I received a letter via the internal despatch system that I had at last passed my initial police driving course. Vauxhall Motors being based in Dunstable meant that Bedfordshire and Luton Constabulary had a fleet of nice new HC Viva 'Panda' cars and my first day of being a solo area patrol driver was a proud one indeed. Of course, the excitement wasn't due to last.

During my first week I was answering an emergency call and halfway between Dunstable and the village of Eaton Bray, I got a puncture. In addition to some heavy rain at the time, my Pye pocketphone radio refused to transmit and on top of that I'd rushed from the station and left my issue Gannex raincoat behind. So not only was I unable to let local Control know I couldn't get to the burglary in progress, it was raining in torrents and I had a puncture to repair. Fortunately, the vehicle's main force radio system was working so I was able to alert Police Headquarters (and every other patrol car in the county) to the fact that I had a puncture and couldn't respond to the burglary shout. To rub salt in the wound, two officers in the A5 traffic patrol car that was diverted to the incident arrested the burglar who was still in possession of stolen jewellery just a few hundred yards from the scene. But at least he was caught and subsequently admitted a whole series of similar daytime house burglaries; just a shame I drove over a nail at the wrong time.

One of the small pleasures of being a qualified police driver was getting to drive all manner of vehicles, including, on occasions, high-end stolen cars. One day I was dropped off at Houghton Regis at the site of an abandoned Mercedes sedan, stolen from Surrey. Armed with the largest bunch of car keys in the world, my task was to drive the beast back to the police station for fingerprinting and subsequent return to the owner. Sitting in the driver's seat I realised I was about to drive a car with an automatic gear box. This was a first for me as police driver training, excellent though it was, did not include automatics. Still, how hard could it be with no manual gear lever and no clutch to worry about? Apparently, all you had to do was keep your left foot out of the way.

Eventually I got the very impressive V8 engine started, released the handbrake and gingerly pressed the accelerator, moving smoothly forward out of the car park and heading carefully towards Dunstable. This was easier than imagined and I remember thinking what an amazing car it was to drive, the ultimate in style and comfort. I glided to a halt at the High Street North/Houghton Road crossroads traffic lights, intending to turn left into the high street. Waiting for the lights to turn green, I couldn't hear the engine ticking over above the sound of Black Sabbath blasting from the car's intricate eight track stereo system, the volume control of which was nowhere to be seen.

To make sure the engine hadn't cut out, I booted the throttle so I could hear the revs, completely forgetting it was an automatic and in 'drive' mode. The engine roared and we shot like a cork from a bottle, rocketing across the junction against the still red traffic light. With no time to turn the wheel, all I could do was steer the thing in as straight a line as possible and manoeuvre into Brewers Hill Road directly opposite. The road accident gods were indeed smiling that day and I have no idea how I avoided a collision with the cross flow of traffic, although there was a motorcyclist who must have needed a change of underwear after swerving around the back end of the Merc. I accelerated away, pretending I was on some sort of emergency and hoping against hope that anyone who had witnessed the incident didn't report it. Fortunately for me, no one did.

On another occasion I wasn't quite so lucky. On single crewed mobile patrol during a set of nights I was called to a 999 serious accident in the town centre. It was around 1 am and I was half a mile away on Dunstable's southbound carriageway, so it was on with the blue light (no sirens on divisional vehicles in those days) and a quick U-turn to get back to the town. At least, that was the plan. Halfway through the U-turn there was an almighty bang and a jolt with the sound of grinding metal as an MGB GT sports car embedded itself in the police car's rear passenger door. There was a long silence then all hell broke out. As I clambered out of the driver's seat, I was aware of a female running up and down the pavement screaming hysterically. I ran round to the driver's door of the MG and saw the driver slumped over the steering wheel. He stirred as I approached and I helped him out of the car; thankfully he was relatively uninjured. The female was his passenger and although suffering from shock, also escaped any significant injury. I received a headache and a very bruised ego.

The accident resulted in both the MGB driver and myself being convicted, me for careless driving and him for bombing along at excess speed. Being then suspended from driving police vehicles for two months, it was back on the beat for me, carrying out town centre foot patrol during the day and shaking hands with doorknobs on nights. But fair to say that one particular burglar wouldn't have been caught if I'd been in a patrol car.

Chapter 6

Burglaries and a Breathalyser

The sound of muffled footsteps came from somewhere on the rooftops of the buildings overlooking the high street. As it was 2 am, it definitely needed investigating, so having pinpointed the sound to be coming from the vicinity of Woolworths' roof, I quietly radioed in for assistance before slipping down a side alley and climbing carefully up a fire escape onto the flat roof. There I had my first encounter with a young man called Danny, already well known in local police circles as having a yearning for the goods and chattels of others.

We literally bumped into each other as Danny headed for the fire escape I had just vacated, the difference being he hadn't expected to meet a policeman whereas I had expected to meet someone up to no good. Having the advantage of surprise allowed me to sweep his legs from under him, kneel on his back and handcuff both wrists together. Not as difficult as you might think as Danny was just twelve years old, but despite his small frame and tender years he was an experienced and prolific office breaker.

That night he'd broken into a solicitor's office via a skylight and stolen three pens, a paperweight and a packet of sweets, all of which were recovered from his pockets. In subsequent years I was to have a few 'professional' meetings with Danny, but our last encounter was some thirty-five years following on from that first tussle on Woolworths' roof. Some years following my retirement, I walked into a local pub with my wife and found myself standing at the bar next to a giant of a man who constantly stared at me. Eventually he said, "You was the filth, weren't you?"

Any retired police officer in this situation knows instinctively that the next couple of minutes will go one of two ways.

"Do I know you?"

"You should. Danny Griffin."

It instantly dawned, and despite the other dealings I'd had with him, my mind went back to that night on the rooftop. So did his.

"Well, well," I said, "would never have recognised you."

"No, a bit bigger than the nipper you threw about on the roof that night," he said, stone-faced. Here we go, I thought. Then he grinned and moved away from the bar to join his mate at a table. I breathed a sigh of relief that retribution wasn't on his mind.

Back in 1974, my temporary driving ban eventually ended and once more I was a patrol driver. Dunstable's police station in High Street South was purpose built in 1930 with one of its innovative features being a control centre for an intruder activation system with no audible activation at the site of the protected premises to warn a burglar. There were, of course, many false alarms but one particularly reliable system was installed at a local sports club situated on the edge of a housing estate a mile or so from the town centre. There had been two previous alarm activations resulting in arrests on both occasions so when an intruder alert for the premises came over the radio at 12.30 am one morning, the adrenaline kicked in.

At the time, I had a newly appointed constable riding shotgun over my week of nights, an excitable young fellow called Charlie. Being the town centre mobile meant we were first to arrive in the vicinity and as we approached the turning to the club I drove slowly along the street without lights and parked in the shadows. We quietly walked towards the premises driveway when suddenly the roar of a motorcycle engine ripped through the night air accompanied by a single headlight travelling at speed from the club driveway in our direction. Charlie was a few yards ahead of me and promptly leapt into the road signalling the motorbike to stop, which it didn't. Now roaring towards me, I instinctively stuck my fist out. The rider was wearing an open face helmet and I felt a jarring crunch as my fist slammed into his face. He toppled backwards off the bike, rolled over and came to rest in the gutter almost at Charlie's feet whilst the motorcycle careered off down the road before wrapping itself around a lamp post. What was it with me and lamp posts?

Charlie was all over the hapless and injured motorcyclist like a rash and formally arrested him on suspicion of burglary. However, the reply after caution that was screamed at Charlie told its own story: "You stupid tossers, I'm the f......g keyholder!"

Our 'prisoner' was indeed the keyholder and had accidentally set off the alarm whilst securing the clubhouse; he failed to stop for Charlie because he hadn't seen him in time.

He suffered three smashed teeth, several facial lacerations and a hairline fracture of the nose. Plus, a motorbike that was a write off. My default resignation mindset following job related disasters returned with a vengeance, particularly when the Force Complaints and Discipline department descended.

Under the Police (Discipline) Regulations 1965, we were both served notices which explain the offence or matter for which you are under investigation. This was to be expected, notwithstanding we were trying to apprehend a suspected burglar, I had still assaulted an innocent member of the public. The worry was that if it was found that I had acted unreasonably then a criminal charge of causing Actual Bodily Harm (or worse) could be brought.

A stressful time in my new career, and by no means to be the last. Fortunately, the injured motorcyclist did agree that he was driving perhaps a little too quickly to have safely stopped for Charlie's signal and therefore was at least partly responsible for what happened. Thankfully, he made a full recovery and I was eventually exonerated.

The next burglar alarm I was sent to a few weeks later ended with a better result. Again on nights, the alarm at Dunstable Town Football Club activated. It was the early hours again and I arrived at the edge of the club car park at the same time as the shift dog handler. One man and his dog plus me tiptoed through the darkness towards the single storey premises. We could hear movement inside and as there were no internal lights on, it was a pretty good guess that some form of villainy was afoot. The door was partly open and the padlock hanging off. The dog man's shouted warning, "Come out now or the dog comes in!" resulted in a swift and wise response. Two teenage burglars emerged one after the other and were duly arrested. For the second time – and on many more occasions throughout my career – the value of well-trained dogs in so many avenues of police work became obvious. Not only in the detention of suspects but in the search for drugs and explosives as well as locating missing persons and finding crime scene evidence.

Never knowing what we would be faced with whilst on mobile patrol, police cars were always double crewed when resources allowed, although more often than not, resources didn't allow it. Such was the case one Saturday morning when I was on solo patrol driving through the village of Toddington when I saw a mk3 Cortina pull out of a turning ahead of me and speed away. I didn't know why at the time, but something wasn't right.

The car had a number of occupants and given its sudden acceleration was certainly worthy of a stop check. I radioed the vehicle index number through to the force control room, but being aware of the length of time such a check would take, I resolved to stop the car and hope to establish the existence or otherwise of any offences.

Today, officers can establish everything about a suspect vehicle within seconds of a radio check via the Police National Computer (PNC), but in the early seventies such checks were laboriously carried out by telephone from the local police headquarters control room to the Central

Vehicle Index (CVI) at New Scotland Yard (NSY). This was a manual check and of course even if a vehicle had been reported stolen it may not yet have been entered onto the CVI system, creating a negative result.

I caught up with the Cortina, now travelling at 60 mph towards the village of Houghton Regis. With blue light activated, I flashed the driver to pull over. He eventually did so and the car jolted to a stop on the grass verge. For a police patrol officer the following ten seconds are crucial in a vehicle stop check scenario for that is the time you are most likely to come unstuck; once out of the car you are more vulnerable to assault, or the subject vehicle could accelerate away. To my surprise, all four occupants remained in the vehicle and the driver wound his window down, smiling amiably as I approached.

"Morning officer," he greeted. "Everything OK?"

The vehicle was nearly new and with the best will in the world, it just didn't go together with its teenage occupants, something was definitely amiss.

"Morning," I said. "Is this your car?"

"Certainly is."

"What's the registration number?"

"Not sure, only had it a couple of weeks."

"Driving licence please?"

The driver reached into his inside pocket and produced a licence. They didn't contain a photograph of the owner in those days so there was no immediate way of checking its authenticity. I asked for his date of birth and the answer he gave matched the one on the licence.

My objective now was to play for as much time as possible and hope for a response from the control room before too much longer. I began to question the passengers, two male and a female, and having received some monosyllabic responses to most of my queries I returned to the police car on the pretext of checking out matey's driving licence.

As I got to the car, the force VA radio crackled into life, "Can you speak, Delta 8?"

"Go ahead."

"Grab the keys, vehicle stolen from Ilford."

"Received, vehicle's four up so assistance required."

"In hand, Delta 8, van from Dunstable en route to you."

With assistance being at least five minutes away, my priority was to prevent the car and at least the driver from making an escape. I casually walked back to the Cortina and handed the licence back to the driver. "Seems to be in order," I said, and as he returned the licence to his pocket, I reached through the window and yanked the keys from the ignition.

"Stay in the car, all of you. You're in a stolen vehicle and you're under arrest."

Not sure exactly what I expected to happen next, but what did occur certainly surprised me.

"OK mate, you got us," declared the driver, "and you might want to look in the back."

The boot was full of electrical equipment and assorted items, all proceeds of burglaries as well as a series of thefts from garden centres across north London.

The driving licence had come from one of the burglaries and my driver had memorised the date of birth and address of the owner. It seems the group had embarked on a three-day crime spree simply for the hell of it and with no real end game. I had stopped them at the point where they were exhausted and bored...

The four prisoners were taken to Dunstable Police Station whilst preliminary enquiries were carried out after which they were collected by the Met and taken to one of the North London stations to be dealt with as the majority of offences had been committed within the Metropolitan Police district. Although the job didn't do much for Bedfordshire's crime detection figures, the Met were over the moon as they managed to clear up a whole series of thefts and office burglaries across London from Ilford to Wembley.

Speaking of the collection of prisoners from other areas, an interesting episode concerned a colleague who went to collect a prisoner from a police station situated, shall we say, somewhere in a rural location in the Cotswolds. The prisoner had been arrested on a warrant issued in Luton and was awaiting collection by Bedfordshire. My colleague and a fellow officer arrived at the little police station and parked their unmarked vehicle in the rear yard. Unable to access the building from the yard they walked out onto the street and followed the footpath to the front until they came to a small garden gate which let them onto a lovely, manicured path leading to the front door of the police station. There were well-tended bushes on one side of the path and a pristine lawn on the other, a garden to be proud of in any location but especially belonging to a police station. The idyllic scene was enclosed within a lovely Cotswold stone wall, all a far cry from the enormous brick edifice of Luton Police Station from whence they came. The station gardener was hard at work tending the lawn with his constabulary Suffolk Colt lawnmower and waved a cheery welcome to the officers as they walked up the path. What a difference to what they were used to, a more welcoming constabulary scenario was difficult to imagine. Once inside the station they were met by the Duty Sergeant.

"Morning Sergeant, we're here to collect George Jones, I have a warrant to take him back to Luton."

"No problem," replied the Sergeant, "I'll get his property for you."

He reached into a cupboard behind him and retrieved a bag which he placed on the table in front of him and emptied out the contents: a comb, wallet, two photographs, a packet of cigarettes and some loose change. The Sergeant counted it all out and asked my colleague to sign for the property and the prisoner.

"I can see the property is all there as recorded on your detention sheet, but I need to see the prisoner before I sign and for him to agree his property?"

"OK, but it's all there."

"I don't doubt it, but I do need to see the prisoner before I sign."

Muttering under his breath, the Sergeant came around the table, brushed past the two officers and opened the station entrance door. He stood on the threshold and shouted, "George, can you stop mowing for a minute and come in here, there's two policemen from Luton for you." Alas, there were no gardens at Luton Police Station for George to look after.

Arrests whilst on mobile patrol came thick and fast in the early seventies and ranged from offences of disqualified driving, car theft and assault to burglary, robbery and drink driving. Much the same as today, I'm guessing!

One day, a jewellery snatch occurred at one of the town centre shops where the offenders had grabbed a tray of rings from the counter and assaulted a shop assistant who tried to stop them leaving. They were chased into a car park by two members of the public who managed to take the registration number of their vehicle as they sped off towards the town centre. The car was stopped ten minutes later and both men arrested. Meanwhile, myself and a colleague attended the shop to take statements and establish any witnesses.

If ever I wondered about the usefulness of long weeks spent memorising various pieces of statute and legal definitions at the police training centre, then, on this occasion, I wondered no longer. The offenders were in custody and would be charged at some point, but what exactly would they be charged with?

This was pre-CPS of course and charging decisions were made solely by the police usually without reference to a solicitor, which made it of crucial importance that the evidence gathered was accurate and pertinent. As I began to take a written statement from the staff member who had been assaulted, I was wrestling in my mind with the components of the robbery definition under the Theft Act 1968. It was a thin line between an offence of robbery and one of straight theft plus assault as it all depended on when the assault took place.

Strange, but even today, fifty years on, the definition remains clear in my memory:

A person is guilty of robbery if he steals, and immediately before or at the time of doing so, and in order to do so, he uses force on any person or puts or seeks to put any person in fear of being then and there subjected to force.

The importance of accurate charging is paramount, not least because a theft conviction on indictment carries a maximum tariff of seven years whilst robbery at the top end of the scale can result in a possible life sentence. In this case, the offender had punched a staff member in the face as he fled through the doorway into the street. Technically, the theft had occurred and was completed before the assault took place, therefore the offence seemed to be one of theft with an additional charge of assault.

When the case eventually came to trial at Bedford Crown Court, a long legal argument surrounded the issue of precisely when the physical offence of theft had ended. After direction by His Honour Judge Lymbery QC that in this particular case it was effectively a continuing offence, the jury found both defendants guilty of robbery. You live and learn.

Coincidentally, a year later I found myself again in front of Judge Lymbery with a defendant in a breathalyser case who had resisted arrest and assaulted me whilst trying to escape from his vehicle. He'd crashed into – you guessed it – a lamp post.

At the conclusion of the trial at Bedford Crown Court and the subsequent conviction of my defendant on all charges, Judge Lymbery asked me to demonstrate to the jury how the breathalyser kit was assembled and used. Now the only thing more stressful than a Crown Court cross examination is being unexpectedly recalled to the witness box. Anything can happen, and of course, it did.

The breathalyser kit in those days consisted of a series of sealed glass tubes filled with green crystals; the ends of the tube were snapped off, a plastic bag attached to one end and a mouthpiece to the other. The motorist was required to blow deeply into the bag and if his breath turned the crystals yellow, it was a positive test resulting in arrest. The glass tubes were housed in a green plastic box which contained a serrated section to allow the tube ends to be snapped off. So, there I was in the witness box with my glass breathalyser tube ready to demonstrate its use to the court. I hacked off one of the ends, attached the bag and began to snap off the opposite end of the tube when, to my horror, it slipped through my fingers. As if in a slowed down film sequence, it hit the lid of the green box which was resting on the edge of the witness box and the entire kit fell into the well of the court.

As I stared down at the shattered box and glass fragments splattered across the floor, I was aware of the abject silence and of the judge, jury, counsel, solicitors, clerk of the court, police colleagues, reporters, ushers and members of the public all staring at me. One of the golden rules of giving evidence under cross examination is to 'never fill the silence' but this was different.

"Sorry about that, your honour," I mumbled.

"Not to worry officer." replied Judge Lymbery, then uttering the words I really didn't want to hear, "Shall we try again?"

Another breathalyser kit was brought into court and to my relief the kit this time was successfully assembled. The judge suggested that to complete the demonstration, someone should blow into the bag. I swear there was a twinkle in his eye when he said, "Perhaps learned counsel for the defence, Mr. Smith, would care to inflate the bag?"

Mr Smith's face was a picture. But what could he do? He duly inflated the bag and an usher handed it back to me. Before I could dispose of the tube, the judge enquired, "Officer, is there any reading?"

The reading was a resounding positive result and, on the street, would have resulted in the arrest of the learned counsel.

"Yes, your honour, it's positive."

"A good job we're not driving today then, Mr Smith," smiled the judge. It was early afternoon and His Honour undoubtedly suspected that Mr Smith had enjoyed something of a liquid lunch. Or maybe he knew he had. But at least it had drawn attention away from my witness box clumsiness.

In 1974, I applied and was elated to be selected to join the Criminal Investigation Department (CID) at Dunstable as an 'aide'. This was a major personal event for me, something I regarded as a turning point in my career and I really needed to make it work. The CID aide system was a period of usually four months where one joined the department as a temporary detective officer, being expected to investigate reported crime, deal with prisoners and prepare files for court. Supervisory officers could then assess the aide's suitability for the role with a view to his/her subsequent appointment as a Detective Constable (DC). Today, there are multiple ways of becoming a detective officer, including in most forces, by direct entry. Providing applicants have a minimum 2:2 undergraduate degree from a UK university, they can enter a two-year National Detective Programme, at the end of which the student has the option of continuing as a full-time detective or leaving the force to pursue a preferable career. I tend to agree with a comment by DI Jack Regan in an episode of *The Sweeney* during a discussion on how the CID was changing, "Bleedin' good job I was born when I was, George."

My secondment to the CID was certainly a case of being thrown in at the deep end; a horrific murder had been committed at Leighton-Linslade and much of Bedfordshire's CID strength was seconded to the enquiry. Seventy-seven-year-old Elsie Claydon was stabbed to death at her home and despite a massive investigation including prolonged nationwide enquiries and appeals, the murder remained undetected. In August 1981, Leighton Buzzard was shocked by a further brutal killing when thirty-six-year-old Carol Morgan was hacked to death in the shop she owned with her husband in Finch Crescent. Again, the offender was not caught, but both files remain open and detailed cold case reviews are conducted every two years to examine fresh information and re-examine existing data.

During the investigation into the Claydon murder I remained as one of a handful of detective officers left to deal with the day-to-day reported crime and our normal workload trebled, as did the overtime. In those days, police officers were not paid for their hours of work after a normal eight-hour tour of duty although CID officers did receive a Detective Duty Allowance for which they had to work at least one hundred and fifty six hours overtime in every quarter. It's fair to say that even under normal circumstances everyone's workload more than qualified for the allowance.

However, in the late seventies the pay ethos of the police service underwent a dramatic change for the better when Lord Edmund-Davies was appointed to chair a commission of enquiry into the negotiating machinery for police pay and conditions.

In 1979 his recommendations were implemented in full, resulting in a pay increase of around 45 per cent, making the Service competitive and a far more attractive career.

Chapter 7

A Detective at Last

Coincidentally, it was Edmund-Davies who had been the presiding judge at the Great Train Robbery trial. The infamous crime took place on 8th August 1963 just three miles from Leighton Buzzard when £2.6 million was stolen from the Glasgow to London mail train. The thirty-year sentences created widespread criticism but other observers were of the opinion that the tariff imposed upon them was correct and penalties for crimes such as murder, rape and terrorism etc. should be correspondingly higher. The debate rumbles on.

Owing to staff shortages brought about by the Claydon murder enquiry, my CID secondment was arguably the hardest period of my career to date in terms of volume of work. Local crime levels remained the same as they were prior to the murder but with a fraction of the resources to deal with them. The cells were generally full with prisoners from overnight arrests 'left for CID to deal with' and the process tended to become a regular exercise: beginning the day at 8 am and reading up witness statements relating to which prisoner(s) were allocated to you by the Detective Sergeant (DS). This would probably be followed by a visit to the crime scene, organising any searches with the authority of a warrant and if necessary, arranging for the attendance of a duty solicitor to represent the prisoner.

An interview under caution would be carried out, after which you took the prisoner's photograph followed by taking his/her fingerprints. The latter was a skill in itself in those days, each finger and thumb being rolled carefully on a copper ink pad and then onto a form, making sure to create a square image of the print. Sounds simple but if the prisoner was   uncooperative or even nervous and couldn't relax his hands, then it was an exasperating and time-consuming experience. A double set of prints was required for each hand, plus palmprints: one set for the local Force Fingerprint Bureau and a second for the NSY national index, a total of twenty-two prints in all for every prisoner.

Finally, depending on the evidence, the prisoner would be formerly charged and either bailed to appear at court or in certain cases remanded in custody. If there was insufficient evidence to charge him at that time, he could be bailed to appear back at the police station pending further enquiries.

Once the prisoner had been dealt with, the mountain of paperwork you were left with formed the basis of your file. Then on to the next one. If no further prisoners that day, carry on with your own enquiries into the never diminishing pile of undetected crime reports. That was in addition to taking reports of crime over the phone coming into the office from members of the public. I took one such call early in my secondment which began as the theft of a credit card but over the following six months developed into a major fraud investigation involving other cards and thousands of pounds worth of goods obtained across London and the home counties. We tracked down the culprits to their home in Dunstable, and on entering the house, instantly recognised a huge number of stolen items the credit card companies had listed for us. The young couple had virtually kitted out their home on the proceeds of stolen credit cards as well as – on their days off – enjoying the occasional shoplifting spree. On being arrested, the female half commented, "We knew you'd be here sooner or later." Which makes you wonder why they bothered. Thrill of the chase maybe? Whatever, they obviously thought it was worth the risk of imprisonment.

My CID attachment was an unrelenting time with a sharp learning curve, but it was the very reason I joined the job and I loved it. Owing to the murder, my four-month secondment became almost a year, at the conclusion of which, to my huge relief, I was recommended – pending passing a Junior Detective Training Course – for appointment to the CID. I couldn't wait.

It was 1974 and I was sent to the West Yorkshire Metropolitan Police Detective Training School at Bishopgarth, Wakefield for ten weeks to learn how to be a crime investigator. This was during the period that a wave of bombings was being carried out on the UK mainland by the Provisional IRA with sensitivities being particularly high in Yorkshire following the targeting of a coach carrying military personnel and their families on the M62 motorway. A bomb planted in the luggage hold tore the vehicle apart resulting in the deaths of twelve people, including nine soldiers and two children. So, it should have been no surprise that sitting in a classroom at the detective training school in Wakefield whilst registering our arrival that the sound of a muffled explosion echoed through the building. Not a terrorist attack, simply a careless trainee detective who had left a holdall by the side of his car in the car park. Someone had spotted it and within minutes the Bomb Squad arrived, the holdall was swiftly despatched and the unfortunate trainee promptly sent back to his force.

The course was hard work from a study point of view but there was a great deal of outside input from professionals in many fields of expertise with whom, as crime investigators, we were likely to come into contact. For me, the individuals of greatest interest were a forensic scientist, the No.3 Regional Crime Squad co-ordinator, an officer from the Security Service and a fascinating two hour talk from a Manchester University lecturer in psychiatry on 'The Criminal Mind'.

When schedules allowed, the social scene in Wakefield was certainly diverse. The pubs were excellent and sometimes on our occasional evenings 'off' we would visit the Wakefield Theatre Club to see the likes of Bernard Manning, and strangely, on one occasion, Hughie Green. I don't remember what his act consisted of, but he was heckled by the audience to such an extent that he walked off! A Wakefield legend at the time was a local 'entrepreneur' called Frank Hepworth who owned a fish and chip shop in the city centre which was incredibly popular. We soon realised why. If you walked through one of those coloured beaded curtains, popular in the seventies, at the rear of 'Heppy's Fish and Chips' you found yourself in a small but fully functioning nightclub. On selected nights, Frank himself would be on the little stage fronting his own skiffle band before introducing 'an evening of ladies' cultural dancing'. Although the emphasis was most definitely not on 'culture', every Wednesday night 'Heppy's Fish and Strip' as it was known, was jam-packed. Frank was a larger-than-life character and a very funny man who must have made a fortune from his venture which lasted well into the 1980s. Although some of our 9 am classroom sore heads were down to Frank and his Tetley's bitter, none of us would have missed the 'northern culture' experience.

Six weeks into the course, disaster struck. The one thing I had dreaded. For the first time in five years, the virus reactivated the ulcer on my eye with a vengeance and the pain was worse than I had previously experienced. At Wakefield Hospital, I went through the iodine cauterisation ordeal once again and the eye remained bandaged for the next two weeks. The course instructor, kindly but firmly, said my options were to try and catch up on the law lectures I had missed and hope for the best in the final exams or return to my force to recover. For me it was a no-brainer, I did not want to be re-coursed (even if there was another vacancy, which couldn't be guaranteed) so I decided to remain and do my best to qualify. It was a very difficult two weeks. In some pain and finding concentration really demanding, I struggled to catch up on what I'd missed as well as trying to take in the current lessons. This was what I had strived for ever since I could remember and I wasn't about to give up. The results of the final exams were eventually revealed and nobody was more astonished than me to learn that I had scraped through them all, in a couple of cases literally with a single mark the right side of the pass line. I have no idea if allowances had been made for my illness; for the sake of my self-respect, I like to think not, but realistically, I couldn't see how I could have made up almost two weeks of course work in just a few days. Whether my good fortune was due to the instructors or to providence, I'll never really know, but either way, it meant I was now qualified, pending a vacancy, to become a fully accredited detective officer. I was on cloud nine.

Once back home, my eye began to recover and although the ulcer had caused additional scarring to the cornea resulting again in a very small percentage of sight loss, it did not make a significant difference to my overall vision in terms of distance or close-up. Thank God. However, there were no immediate vacancies within the CID at the time, so I returned to uniform patrol duties to await appointment.

Despite the affection Lynda and I had for our first home together at the Toddington police house, we wanted our own property and having managed to secure a mortgage we bought a small new-build three-bedroom house in Dunstable for £10,650. Everything is pro-rata of course, but strange to think that today that amount of money would hardly buy a third share in a south coast beach hut.

At that time, one of the necessities for a uniformed constable to be considered for a post in the CID was that he/she must have passed the promotion examination to Sergeant to prevent a 'log jam' of unqualified Detective Constables with nowhere to progress. In practice, the officer would normally serve a minimum of two years as a DC and would then, subject to passing a promotion board interview, be eligible for promotion to uniform Sergeant. My sole ambition was to be a detective officer and I had no inclination to return to uniform, in whatever rank. To me, the exam was a necessary evil to get what I wanted so I studied hard, sat the exam and was fortunate enough to pass. On 1st April 1975, six months after my return from Wakefield, my greatest ambition was realised when I was appointed Detective Constable. It would have been an enormous relief to me had I been aware that over the next twenty-seven years of service I would never return to uniform duties.

I thoroughly enjoyed working in the CID office: my own caseload, carrying out investigations at the time and speed I wanted, detecting offences and interviewing witnesses and of course, prisoners. The only downside for me was attendance at court, always the big unknown and although I was to give evidence countless times at every tier of criminal court in the land, my antipathy of the process never diminished.

For a comparatively small market town with a population of 30,000 or so, in terms of crime, Dunstable was a surprisingly busy place. I'd been in my new job less than a week when an emergency call came in that an armed robbery was taking place at the Midland Bank in West Street. Patrol officers were on route and the four of us in the CID office at the time rushed to the vehicle key board to grab a car. Only one set of keys was available so we all piled into the unmarked Vauxhall Viva in the rear yard to get to the scene as quickly as we could – the bank was less than half a mile away, so we'd be there fairly quickly. And if the car hadn't had a flat battery, we would have made it. Pushing and shoving each other out of the car, we ran from the police station to the bank. By the time we got there, breathless and red-faced, the robbers had of course made good their escape along with £196,000. I wasn't involved in the follow-up investigation but several months on, with assistance from the Metropolitan Police Flying Squad, the offenders were subsequently identified, prosecuted and imprisoned. But I clearly remember the rollicking we got that day from the DI on arrival back at the station.

"What the f… were you lot playing at?" I thought his annoyance was due to leaving the CID office unoccupied or maybe allowing an operational vehicle to be left with a flat battery. No, neither of those things.

"Why did you charge on foot into an armed robbery situation with no plan, no back up and not tell anyone what you were doing?" he shouted angrily.

"Well, they'd gone when we got there, governor," one of our number said, lamely.

"Bloody good job for you," he yelled, "else the lot of you could have been shot! Clue's in the name you f......morons, ARMED robbery!" He was right of course, we were two new DCs and a couple of CID aides but we should have known better; it was unfortunate there was no DS in the office at the time to put the brakes on us.

Crimes passed to the CID to be dealt with were many and varied, including serious assaults, sexual offences, office break-ins, robberies and fraud. One of the most prevalent and always prioritised offences was that of house burglary; Bedfordshire is an essentially rural county within easy travelling distance of London and as such, is home to some large and attractive properties situated in many of the smaller villages. The M1 motorway, A1, A5 and A6 run through the county, providing easy access for criminals wishing to take advantage of rapid exit routes.

During the summer of 1977 a series of 'burglary dwellings' began around the south Bedfordshire villages of Whipsnade, Studham and Kensworth and as I was already investigating the first reported burglary, I became the Officer in the Case (OIC) for the series. The modus operandi (MO) of the offences was invariably the same: carried out in the daytime whilst the occupiers were away, entry usually by smashing a small window at the rear of the premises, a methodical search of the house was conducted and jewellery, silverware and any smaller items of value were stolen. The SOCOs were of the opinion that the offender(s) wore gloves throughout.

I carried out extensive house to house enquiries around the villages over many hours, often requiring evening work to catch people at home. Along with colleagues, we organised interviews of postmen, tradespeople and as many delivery drivers that we could trace in an effort to find anyone that may have seen something to provide the lead we needed. The burglaries were being committed once every two or three weeks, sometimes over a weekend, and despite increased patrols and observations around the villages, the thief or thieves continued to evade capture. I was now investigating six linked burglaries over that summer and the only piece of information I had to go on was that a silver Mercedes saloon car had been seen driving through the area on two separate days when offences had been committed. There was no registration number nor a description of the driver, but it was something. On the off-chance that the offender might have needed some Dutch courage prior to carrying out his activities, I arranged for all eight pubs situated in the three villages to be visited and the sparse details of the Mercedes car were left with the licensees with a request that if such a vehicle appeared in their car park during the daytime, to telephone me immediately. A long shot but worth trying.

Two weeks later, I was at home enjoying a rare midweek rest day when the office rang.

"John? Sorry, you're needed in." The DS sounded excited.

"What's up?"

"We've got your man in custody."

I had to admit that my instant jubilation at this news was tempered with disappointment that I hadn't been there at the kill, as it were. Weeks of hard work had culminated in this moment and I was on my day off! But the hard work had indeed been worthwhile; the licensee of one of the pubs had rung my office extension to report that he had a stranger in the bar drinking a large Scotch who had arrived in a silver Mercedes.

"Get here quick," the landlord had whispered down the phone, "not sure how long he'll be here."

Two of my CID colleagues jumped into a car and arrived at the pub ten minutes later, the Mercedes still being present in the car park and the suspect about to finish his drink. He could not supply the registration number of his car to my colleagues and was reluctant to open the boot, inside which was discovered a jemmy, a number of screwdrivers, two pillowcases and significantly, a single gold earring. He was arrested on suspicion of burglary and detained at the station ready for me to deal with him.

The Mercedes had been stolen from Heathrow airport some three months earlier and it turned out that our man was wanted across the home counties and by the Metropolitan Police for many similar burglaries, the theft of a number of performance vehicles, countless hotel and credit card fraud offences as well as prolific thefts from golf clubs.

Something of a political argument ensued concerning which police force should have precedence of investigation and therefore take responsibility for collating the multitude of crimes this man had committed. Bedfordshire stuck to their guns and retained the right to deal with the prisoner from interviews through to eventual prosecution, which meant that the next two months or so of my professional life were set. Being a comparative novice in dealing with crime investigation at this level, I needed some help and this was adequately supplied by DS George Prior, an experienced DS from whom I learned a great deal, but more of George later.

The prisoner was remanded in cell custody and the following days were taken up by extensive interviews with him concerning my six house burglaries, details of the property stolen and how and where he had disposed of it. He fully admitted everything, in addition to which, forensic evidence from the stolen Mercedes, including the gold earring, provided conclusive proof of his guilt in relation to the Bedfordshire offences. I sent a teleprinter message to all forces giving the offender's identity, the type of crimes of which he was suspected and his usual MO. The response was rapid with an abundance of replies from many police areas, following which we formulated an appointments system allowing arrangements to be made for officers from the interested forces to come along to interview him relating to similar outstanding crimes in their areas. He confessed to many, but not all; as time progressed, he tended to admit to only those where he believed there was some degree of evidence against him. At the conclusion of the investigation, he pleaded guilty to a total of ten specimen charges on the indictment at St Albans Crown Court and asked for one hundred and fifteen similar offences to be taken into consideration (TIC) and was sentenced to five years' imprisonment. A major learning event for me and my first experience of carrying out a full investigation from the first report of a serious crime to identifying the offender and collating and preparing the prosecution evidence for the subsequent trial. It was quite a buzz to know that my basic investigatory legwork had led to catching a professional criminal and bringing him to justice. It was exactly why I had joined the police and I wanted more of that feeling.

It was a busy time in the CID during the seventies and offenders appearing before the local magistrates' court were all prosecuted by the police unless the offence was of a particularly complex nature, in which case a solicitor would probably be employed to conduct the trial. The CPS was not formed until 1986 so charging advice from a solicitor was rarely sought and any prisoners in the cells were not routinely subject to court scrutiny. Given the views of my Detective Chief Inspector (DCI) boss at the time, this was just as well. One Friday afternoon I arrested one of our local prolific offenders for a series of office break-ins: an eighteen-year-old who was decidedly uncooperative. He was placed in a cell to cool off whilst I considered my next move. Work permitting, 6 pm on a Friday was something of an unofficial 'weekly debrief' session for any detectives in the office at the time. It was invariably led by the DCI and necessarily involved adjourning to the Saracens Head pub across the road. When I told the boss I was busy with a prisoner and would miss this week's debrief, the conversation went thus:

"What's he in for?"

"Office burglaries, governor."

"Is he havin' 'em?"

I shook my head. "Not so far."

"Then bugger him, he can stew, the debriefs are important."

"But I'm off for the weekend sir, I need to crack on and deal with him tonight, the Station Sergeant's already asking what's happening with him."

"Listen lad," said the DCI sharply, "cells are the only aid to interrogation we have, he can reflect over the weekend, and you can sort him out on Monday. I'll square it with the Station Sergeant."

And that's what happened. I spent an apprehensive weekend waiting for a phone call from either Complaints and Discipline or a solicitor threatening a writ of habeas corpus for the immediate release of his client. I went in at 8 am on the Monday and interviewed a greatly subdued burglar who made a full written confession admitting all the break-ins of which he was suspected; he was charged and released on bail to appear at court. If such circumstances were repeated today, it would of course be more likely that I would be the one bailed to go to court. But in those days, it was *Life on Mars*.

Owing to its proximity to the police station, the Saracens Head pub in the high street hosted many CID 'briefings' over the years and when the station closed down in favour of a new, much larger construction in West Street in 1979, allegiance switched to the Queen Victoria pub for which we didn't even have to cross the road – it was situated immediately next door to the station. Many tales have been told about various happenings involving the constabulary at 'the Vic' over the years, some might bear publication, most would not. As everyone knows, during the seventies, pubs and clubs were much more a part of all sections of the community than they are today. Villains had their favoured drinking holes and it was considered part of CID responsibility to discover which they were – knowing who drank where and making allies of as many licensees as possible led to a great deal of useful intelligence. These days of course, digitalised information about anyone and everything is stored somewhere and can be accessed; social media is an integral part of any investigative armoury and rightly so, but on balance I think the policing methods of half a century ago, although sometimes slow and tedious, were quite effective and without doubt infinitely more fun!

Over a period of months, we had been plagued by a series of timber thefts from various building sites in the region. No major quantities were taken at any one time but over a period of weeks the amounts became significant. I had been allocated most of the jobs and the only piece of information I had gained was that a blue Vauxhall Cavalier had been seen leaving one of the sites with the rear seats loaded with wood. Part of a registration number had been taken and it was noted there was considerable damage to the front passenger door. On 16th August 1977, I was on a late evening mobile crime patrol driving down the high street when I saw a blue Cavalier fitting the description, complete with door damage, parked on the side of the road outside a pub. Owing to a darts match that night, the pub was packed and I knew all police units were committed on various jobs around the town, so I had a choice: wait for an hour for the pub to turn out or try and resolve it now. So, I walked into the heaving pub, found a space near the door and yelled as loud as I could, "Whose is the blue Cavalier outside?"

The noise subsided as a crowd of faces turned towards me but, as expected, nobody claimed ownership. This was the point at which my plan would work or hopelessly backfire.

"OK," I shouted again, "Well I've just run into the back of it I'm afraid."

I turned and walked out of the pub and crossed the road to where I'd parked the CID car next to the rear bumper of the Cavalier so that the lack of 'accident' damage couldn't be seen. To my relief, I heard footsteps approaching across the road behind me and a voice said, "It's my motor, mate, what happened?"

"Not your day, I'm afraid," I replied, "I'm a police officer and you're under arrest on suspicion of stealing a quantity of wood."

His face was a picture. Examination of the Cavalier boot revealed a quantity of timber wrapping readily identified as coming from the last reported wood theft two nights earlier.

He pleaded guilty to all offences and received a heavy fine. As I mentioned earlier, it's true to say that we often tend to recall where we were at the time of significant world events, hence the significance of the date I caught my man for the wood thefts. That night I was driving home from the police station in the early hours having completed my shift when the news came over the car radio that Elvis Presley had passed away. Like so many of my generation, having grown up with his music and being a huge fan, I felt a real sense of personal loss.

Chapter 8

'Follow That Car...'

Luck plays a part in any investigative process and I certainly had my fair share over the years. Dunstable and Luton had again been suffering from a number of night-time house burglaries where predominantly jewellery was taken, the majority of the offences being linked forensically to having been committed by the same individual. One afternoon, myself and a colleague were on enquiries around the Hadrian housing estate in Dunstable, taking statements from witnesses concerning a particular incident, when we spotted a local man we both knew well emerging from the side of one of the houses. Alf was an accomplished house breaker in his fifties, 6 foot 5, skinny as a rake and walked with a limp. The Hadrian estate consisted of smart, privately owned houses and was not at all the type of area one would expect Alf to be frequenting, he lived some way away on the other side of the tracks, as it were. We got out of the car.

"Hello lads," he said cheerily as he approached. "How are you?"

"We're fine, Alf," said my mate. "And what are you doing around here?"

"Looking for my dog, he's run off."

"We've been here a while, haven't seen a dog."

"Wonder where he's got to," said Alf, scratching his head.

"Well, whilst you're wondering, turn your pockets out."

"Ah, come on gents," he said, "I'm clean as a bleedin' whistle."

"What's this then?" said my mate, producing a pair of leather gloves and a six-inch screwdriver from Alf's jacket pocket.

"Doing some work for a mate," he mumbled, "forgot they were there."

Alf's reply after caution when we arrested him on suspicion of Going Equipped to Steal was an Ealing film classic: "Gordon Bennett fellers, I'm straight as a die now, wouldn't nick nuffink."

He had slipped through the net as a suspect for the current spate of house burglaries as it was believed he was still serving a two-year term of imprisonment relating to his last conviction. Information on prison releases was not easily obtained and nobody was aware he had been released on licence six weeks earlier. The burglaries fitted Alf's MO completely and the timing of the first in the series coincided with his release from prison. He was subsequently interviewed at the police station by DS George Prior who had previously dealt with him and for whom Alf had a great deal of respect, the end result being a full confession to committing all of the outstanding burglaries including a couple we weren't even aware of. He was remanded in custody until his trial at Bedford Crown Court where he was sentenced to a total of six years' imprisonment.

George Prior had arrived on the division back in 1972 fresh from a secondment to the Regional Crime Squad (RCS) – I mentioned the TV programme *Life on Mars* earlier in relation to the DCI; well, although lower in rank, George was our very own Gene Hunt. A spade was definitely a f…… shovel and if you couldn't drink at least half a dozen pints at every session then you had no business being in the CID. On the RCS he was heavily involved in the enquiry into the notorious Richardson torture gang in south London; some of the stories he related concerning victim testimonies were beyond horrendous, the more documented stories such as the removal of fingers and toes with bolt cutters and the pulling out of teeth with pliers were fairly routine methods of punishment. So, George could have been forgiven for finding our run of the mill CID department somewhat less exciting, but being a

Bedfordshire officer he knew the county and had dealt with many of its criminal fraternity prior to his RCS secondment. Including Alf. At the time of George's arrival at Dunstable in 1972, the house burglary figures over the previous two months were sky high and it was apparent from SOCO that one individual was responsible for the mini crime wave.

George had been in Dunstable for less than a fortnight when he arrested Alf on suspicion of the burglaries, but he denied any involvement and unfortunately there was no direct evidence, forensic or otherwise, to connect him to the offences. George was convinced of Alf's guilt but needed to find evidence, and quickly, or he would have to be released back onto the streets to resume his law-breaking activities. Alf lived with his wife in Houghton Regis and with no chance of searching his home with permission, George needed to get authority quickly before word got around of his arrest. Someone telephoned the clerk of the court with a request to quickly find a local magistrate willing to consider a request for the immediate issue of a search warrant. An hour later, George, along with two DCs from the office and two uniform officers, including me, went along with a handcuffed and belligerent Alf, to his home address to execute the warrant issued under the Theft Act 1968.

We were looking for anything to connect Alf to one or more of the outstanding string of burglaries. After a two-hour search of the house and his garage in a nearby block, we found nothing. The only area not searched so far was a small, dilapidated garden shed, so every effort was made to carry out a minute check of its filthy, spider-infested interior. Still nothing. Alf grinned and said, "Look George, like I said, you got the wrong geezer this time."

Then George spotted the rabbit run at the back of the shed, complete with hutch. "Didn't know you kept rabbits."

"Used to," Alf grunted.

For a rabbit hutch it was quite a palatial affair and very, very secure: it had a little padlock fitted to it!

"So, tell me Alf," said George in anticipation, "when you had rabbits, where did they keep the f...... key?"

Alf's expression confirmed what we were beginning to suspect.

We jemmied off the padlock and it was incredible to see how many items of silverware and jewellery could be packed into a rabbit hutch.

Bingo!

Initially, Alf did 'no comment' interviews but eventually, in an effort to avoid a longer sentence, he admitted five charges of burglary on the indictment, asked for a number of others to be taken into consideration (TIC) and was sentenced to three years' imprisonment.

I found my seven years as a divisional CID officer tremendously rewarding and excellent grounding for the specialist squads I was to join later. I had dealt with – or been involved in the investigation of – many crimes including murder, rape, GBH, aggravated burglary, robbery, fraud and a particularly harrowing case of a serious assault on an eight-month-old baby. That enquiry was carried out by an experienced female officer and myself and I found it an especially difficult investigation to come to terms with. The infant suffered several spiral leg fractures at the hands of his father who was exasperated because the baby wouldn't stop crying. We believed the baby's mother knew what had been going on and kept quiet although we couldn't prove it. I could have cheerfully thrown all 6 foot 3 inches of the father under a bus without a second thought, although justice was more or less done in the end; after a long and protracted enquiry, the father was imprisoned and the child taken into care. I often wonder what became of the little guy.

As with my colleagues, I spent many hours, paid and unpaid, investigating and preparing subsequent case files for court and my home life was pretty sparse, to say the least. Lynda told me how she was once taking our son Mark, aged around five, somewhere in the car with a visiting relative and as they passed the police station, Mark announced, "That's where my daddy lives." Despite my feelings of guilt, the long hours and time spent away from home were not going to improve any time soon.

Some months earlier I had applied to be considered for a post on the Regional Crime Squad (RCS) and in the spring of 1982 I was lucky enough to be seconded to the RCS for a period of three years. Professionally, it was an excellent opportunity and an exciting progression from local crime investigation work to, in the words of its official function, *dealing with those responsible for serious criminal offences which transcend force and regional boundaries.*

The RCS was formed in 1965 and comprised a squad of experienced detectives for each of the nine police districts of England and Wales. It was a successful innovation and remained in its uncomplicated regional format until 1998 when six of the squads amalgamated to become the National Crime Squad (NCS) with responsibility for national and transnational organised and major crime. In 2006 it merged with part of HM Customs and Excise (HMCE) and the National Criminal Intelligence Service (NCIS) to become the Serious Organised Crime Agency (SOCA) dealing with major drug trafficking, contract killings, illegal arms dealing, human trafficking, computer and high-tech crime, money counterfeiting and laundering, extortion, kidnapping and related murders. In 2013, SOCA was replaced by the National Crime Agency (NCA) with similar terms of reference but absorbing the Child Exploitation and Online Protection Centre (CEOPC).

Over the last half century, the UK police service has made astounding transitions in its efforts to combat local, national and international crime and I am proud to have been a part of the earlier days of that process. I hope the ladies and gentlemen so valiantly fighting that battle today enjoy just a fraction of the buzz and the fun we were lucky enough to experience.

The detectives making up each RCS branch office were drawn from the forces of the region they occupied; we were in the Number 5 region so as well as Bedfordshire I was working with officers from Hertfordshire, Thames Valley and Cambridgeshire. Although we generally worked in pairs, I soon learned that the life blood of the RCS – and the primary weapon in its arsenal – was team surveillance work: the art of covertly following one or more individuals on foot or in a vehicle. It is the ultimate in teamwork and requires a great deal of training, practice and application. My surveillance training course at Chelmsford was a revelation and although physically and mentally drained by the end of it, I thoroughly enjoyed learning how to interpret a series of maps whilst travelling at high speed, spending hours following various 'targets' on foot and constantly driving at silly miles an hour in a convoy whilst trying at all times to remain unseen by the suspects. Not easy, but the course and the subsequent live operations I was involved in over the three years of my RCS secondment provided much of the experience and ability that would prove so valuable later in my career.

One thing that surprised me at the time was the absence of any specialist driving instruction – we were expected to drive at breakneck speed in high powered, unmarked cars and, if necessary, ignore traffic lights and warning signs. We would block roundabouts, drive on pavements, grass verges or even across fields, always mindful of not losing the target vehicle and at the same time being aware of the need for public safety. Screaming round London's Hyde Park Corner or the inner ring road in Birmingham or even charging through some tiny hamlet in Devon, was, as a colleague described, the best fun you could have with your clothes on! For the first half of my secondment to the RCS, none of our vehicles were even equipped with two tone sirens which sometimes made things even more interesting.

The teamwork aspect of our mobile surveillance operations was particularly relevant in that you would literally be putting your life – plus those of others in your vehicle – on the line in circumstances, for example, where your convoy was making ground to keep up with a suspect who was travelling at high speed. If you were following a colleague's car who was 'leap frogging' a line of traffic and had negotiated a sharp bend, on seeing the road ahead to be clear of oncoming traffic he would call you through, which meant you were accelerating rapidly around the bend completely blind and on the wrong side of the carriageway. If your mate in the lead car had misjudged the speed of an oncoming vehicle or failed to notice a side turning with a tractor about to pull out, you were of course in real trouble. We each needed to have 100 per cent trust in the ability of everyone else on the team, and for me this was effectively life changing. An only child, I was used to being on my own, making my own decisions and not necessarily having to rely on others. Although with no shortage of close friends and colleagues, I had never before had to physically depend on a team of individuals in the same way that a mobile surveillance operation demanded. If you were not a team player, or failed to rapidly become one, the RCS was not for you.

Quite rightly, things are different today and formal high speed advanced driver training is essential for surveillance operatives as well as many health and safety precautions introduced to keep operatives and the public safe. Even so, the old days were immensely adrenaline fuelled fun! How we got through it without killing a member of the public or one of us, I'll never know, although that's not to say there weren't several hiccups along the way such as damaged wheels, scraped paintwork and the occasional buckled wing. Our office had a friendly body repair garage to hand locally and unless it was obvious the incident had to be reported, the odd dent repair or respray would be rapidly carried out at our own expense; no point in creating unnecessary stress or paperwork, was there?

Immediately following my surveillance course, the first operation I was plunged into concerned a team of criminals based in south London who were carrying out organised night-time burglaries at country houses and churches where silverware, trophies and valuable paintings were stolen to order. The team – in today's parlance, an Organised Crime

Group (OCG) – was also involved in large scale drug dealing and the purchase and distribution of forged Bank of England currency. We received information that on a particular night, two members of the gang were to travel from Stevenage to 'somewhere in Norfolk or Suffolk' where a remote church would be broken into, and a large quantity of silverware stolen. Being aware of the home address of one of the two subjects, we had a starting point for the operation. To mount surveillance on a single individual was a heavy commitment in terms of cost as well as resources and each operation required the involvement of a team with a minimum of a dozen or so officers. The team would remain on duty until the operation was concluded in one of three ways: the subjects were lost/arrested, the Operational Commander (Ops Comm) ended the surveillance, or the subjects failed to commit an offence. With this particular job, the criminals had read the script. Right on schedule, our first subject left his home in Stevenage, picked up criminal number two from the edge of town and then onto the A11 and the A14 to Stowmarket in Suffolk.

As it was now dark, the surveillance process needed to be adapted slightly and although more difficult at night, the major advantage was that we could be so much closer to the subjects in traffic without being seen. On arrival in Stowmarket, our subjects went to a pub, presumably for a calming drink but there was the possibility they could be meeting someone, so their pub visit needed to be closely monitored. One of our team was delegated to enter the pub to observe what our subjects were doing whilst the rest of us 'plotted up' on their vehicle to ensure a smooth resumption of the surveillance once they left. Our man inside reported that the subjects were having a drink at the bar and were not with anyone else. They had several drinks in the pub, returning to their car an hour later. The surveillance resumed and the convoy followed them along dark country roads for what seemed like hours; I was driving one of our Ford Sierras and my co-pilot, an experienced DS, was giving me constant tips and advice during the follow. The time was approaching midnight by now, there was little or no other traffic on the roads and by the limited car to car radio transmissions I could sense the team's collective adrenaline beginning to kick in – we had no idea exactly where or how the subjects were going to carry out their crime, or indeed if they would go ahead with it. But we sensed that whatever was going to happen, or not happen, was imminent.

The convoy lead 'eyeball' car established that the subjects had parked in a secluded gateway without lights and switched off their engine, but the 'eyeball' unit was then committed to pass the targets and until the car at number two back up was in a position to report the movements of our suspects, we were blind to what they were doing and more importantly, where they were. This was the most important part of the operation so far and the most difficult: we were somewhere in the middle of the Suffolk countryside in the dead of night, attempting to observe a pair of criminals commit crime at an unknown location and then arrest them. I couldn't help wondering how the hell this was going to get resolved. The priority was to kill all engine noise and vehicle lighting and to make radio transmissions by covert earpiece only. This meant that any observing of the subjects' movements had to be conducted on foot whilst still maintaining the convoy's ability to instantly follow the target car should it drive off from the gateway. They could have stopped for any reason: perhaps to relieve themselves, look at a map or to see if they were being followed. Or this could be their destination.

Two of our team were trained in covert rural observation tactics and one of them, Jim, was deployed to get as near to the target car as possible to try to confirm the subjects were still in the vehicle. After some ten minutes had passed, a whispered message came over the air, "Subjects not, repeat not, in the vehicle." This was not the news we wanted to hear, in those few minutes we had effectively lost control of our targets and in the darkness on foot we had no hope of establishing their location or direction. But we did have control of their vehicle and our suspects would presumably return to it at some stage, so the convoy settled down to wait. Jim was concealed in undergrowth adjacent to the car, his task being to relay the targets' movements once they were back at the vehicle.

After an hour or so we were jerked into full alert by Jim's subdued but urgent-sounding voice over the radio, "Stand by, stand by!" This meant he had visual contact with one or both targets. If they were back in their vehicle and about to move off, we had to wait for Jim's message that their engine was running before we started up our own vehicles to reduce the risk of them hearing us. Then came a message from Jim that would force our Ops Comm to make an instant and critical decision.

"Subjects both carrying large holdalls, placing them in the boot."

The holdalls could have been empty, or they could contain stolen property, it was too dark for Jim to tell. If we arrested the suspects now and their bags were empty, we had not only blown the surveillance operation, the subjects would probably face, at best, a comparatively minor charge of Going Equipped to Steal. If, on the other hand, we let them run and continued the surveillance to try to identify those receiving the property, we would be taking the risk of losing the targets on the return journey with the added possibility that the holdalls were empty anyway. It was an operational judgement that had to be made within seconds. "Subjects getting into the vehicle," whispered Jim. We needed the decision.

"Strike, strike, strike!"

The instruction came clearly over the radio from the Ops Comm; the signal to move in and arrest. The planning for such an eventuality had been rapidly arranged during the first few minutes of the suspects' absence from their vehicle. One car drove in front of the target, a second hemmed it in from the rear and a third screeched alongside the driver's door. We leapt from our cars, yanked open the doors of the target vehicle and dragged out the two suspects before they could react. Both were held whilst we delved into the two holdalls in the boot: inside were gold candlesticks, plates and chalices. A good call by the Ops Comm. It was mission complete.

The prisoners were taken to the nearest police station and at first light, along with two local DCs, two of our team soon located the church that had been raided. Our prisoners were part of the gang which had been operating for some twelve months across London, the home counties and East Anglia. Our surveillance coincided with other RCS operations resulting in a series of trials at St Albans Crown Court which led to the conviction of twenty-five gang members (including our two) for offences of burglary, drug dealing and possession of forged currency. Each member of our surveillance team was individually commended by the trial judge, His Honour Judge Youds, for our 'tenacity and professional ability' in carrying out the investigation. Although those particular commendations were worthy enough, the funny thing is that police officers often seemed to receive them for the more routine operations and not for work which was probably more deserving. It all depended on the perception of senior officers.

We carried out many covert mobile surveillance jobs involving armed robbery offenders, burglars, major fraudsters and even murder suspects where perhaps additional evidence was required concerning movements or associates. The operations would usually commence within the Number 5 police region but could often end up in towns or cities anywhere in the country. Surveillance led us to Liverpool, Birmingham, Northampton, Brighton, Oxford, Warwick, Cambridge, Bristol, Chelmsford and many others in between, and not surprisingly, most areas of London. Some operations were successful and some, inevitably, were not.

Much depended upon the target's level of awareness in relation to surveillance, the experienced villain being more likely to deploy methods of establishing if he was being followed, such as driving down a dead-end road or doing a sudden U-turn, etc. The problem always for the Ops Comm when this happened was judging whether the target had actually recognised surveillance or was carrying out routine 'just in case' manoeuvres. If the operation was one of intelligence gathering only, then the decision would probably be taken to abort and live to fight another day. If, on the other hand, it was believed a job was live and about to 'go down', such as the commission of a serious crime or the imminent transfer of arms, property, or money, then the chances were we would take the risk and stick with the surveillance whilst preparing, if appropriate, to arrest, disrupt or prevent whatever was about to take place.

It amazes me how we managed to be as successful as we were in the early 1980s, taking into account the almost non-existence of communications between mobile teams and the outside world. Contact was made only via police radio or landline telephone, with mobile phones and even pagers a thing of the future. Conversely, inter-vehicle and person-to-person covert radio technology was quite highly developed even then, enabling us to carry out protracted and otherwise almost impossible surveillance work. But operations rarely went exactly to plan. Take Operation Canberra for example.

The Pines, Goldington Road, Bedford – Force HQ from 1946 to 1978

Eynsham Hall, Oxon, No.5 District Police Training Centre

Class of Summer '69 (wannabe detective is front row, extreme left)

The old Police Station in Friars Walk, Dunstable. Opened in 1929 and remaining as the divisional Police HQ for fifty years, now a funeral parlour

Terry and Police Dog, Zimba

Remains of Charlie Sierra 27

Ulster helicopter patrol, guess who is the shadow on the right, trying not to be ill

A Belfast mural

**Thames House, Westminster, Headquarters of the UK
Security Service**

**85 Albert Embankment, Vauxhall, Headquarters of the UK
Secret Intelligence Service**

Pride of place at home - MI5 shield

Chapter 9

Never Trust a Villain

Operation Canberra was a mobile surveillance commitment against two criminals believed to be travelling from Ipswich to London to 'recce' a National Westminster Bank in preparation for an armed robbery. The operation was carried out at the request of the Metropolitan Police and as neither the location of the bank nor the area of London was known, we needed a full team of personnel to keep tabs on them, especially if they were to split up or meet with associates. We deployed a dozen detectives, both male and female, and a number of vehicles of all descriptions, including a motorcycle. As the final destination of most surveillance operations is rarely known, it is necessary that officers blend in with their surroundings as far as possible when engaged in following targets on foot; it wouldn't make sense for a man in a business suit to follow someone into a rough East End pub, and equally a tramp would draw attention entering a high-end wine bar in Knightsbridge. The class of life of the target is a good starting point but surveillance officers would normally have a change of clothing handy in the car.

The Ipswich targets were successfully picked up – called the 'lift off' – and the surveillance commenced out of the city and south onto the A12 towards Colchester. Our targets were in a silver Ford Sierra and once onto the open road certainly didn't hang about, driving at eighty mph upwards. We were used to following vehicles discreetly at high speed, and it only became an issue when the target reduced speed dramatically for no apparent reason then accelerated again, another ploy to detect possible surveillance. Which is what our Ipswich two did. We knew they could be conscious of surveillance so it was no surprise when they hit the brakes and slowed down to 30 mph for a few miles before slowly going back up to 60 then 70 mph. Soon afterwards without indicating they pulled into a layby and stopped. Our lead 'eyeball' car passed them whilst instructing the convoy to hold back so as not to allow the targets to gain a view of any of the rest of our vehicles. The lead car took the next left turn a mile ahead and positioned itself off the road on a track with a view of the A12. It was a dual carriageway, so our targets had to resume their original southbound route and it was the responsibility of the lead car, the 'eyeball', to give the 'off' as soon as they saw the vehicle pass their view point.

Under normal circumstances, and if our subjects had not been showing signs of looking for surveillance, we would have taken steps to control their movements in the layby by use of a 'bonnet up' vehicle or with a motorcycle pulling in for the rider to eat his sandwiches, etc., but it was deemed too risky with this pair. The crew of the 'eyeball' car ahead also had to make sure once they had given the 'off' that their vehicle remained out of sight of the targets for as long as possible as they had likely been on view for several seconds when passing the layby. Jim and I were at number three in the convoy and on hearing the "Stop" command, we pulled over into a convenient farm gateway some two miles behind the stop to await developments. Less than five minutes later came the message, "Off, off, off, original direction!"

Being at least a couple of miles behind the targets, along with the convoy vehicles positioned at intervals behind us, we needed to make some ground to remain in control of the subjects. Jim was driving our three litre Capri with me on communications and map reading, and as the engine screamed at 5000 revs, I turned up the comms to make sure we missed none of the commentary.

"Target vehicle speed eight zero miles an hour in the offside lane, convoy beware, he is manoeuvring from one lane to another and reducing speed as he does."

Almost every action the Sierra driver had carried out since the 'lift off' in Ipswich had been focused on anti-surveillance movements – whether they had been successful in establishing our presence for certain, only the two of them knew; we had to assume for the time being that they were being ultra-vigilant 'just in case'. Either way, we needed to be on our game with these two. Half an hour later came over the comms:

"All units hold back, it's a stop, stop, stop in the car park of a Little Chef half a mile south of the roadworks!"

Bearing in mind the speeds at which we'd been travelling, the team had to rapidly slow down and either stop somewhere on the A12 as safely as possible or get off the carriageway completely to ensure we did not overshoot the plot. We were the back-up vehicle positioned at number two behind the 'eyeball' car which had been committed to continue past the plot so it was up to Jim and I to take control of the targets. The 'eyeball' car continued commentary:

"All units, the target vehicle has turned around and is parked up facing the entrance so they'll have a visual on the car park entrance, Charlie Sierra 81 beware."

That was us. But before any action was taken a quick decision from the Ops Comm was needed as to which of two options we go for: we all remain away from the Little Chef plot and wait for the subjects to resume their journey so as not to compromise any of the team or we deploy a vehicle into the car park and if necessary, one or more officers on foot into the Little Chef to establish if they were eating and/or meeting a third person.

The intelligence was that the eventual armed robbery for which this was a preliminary recce would be three-handed and the identity of the third individual was unknown. This could be where they were to meet. A DS, Ron, was the Ops Comm on this one and he wasted no time in his instructions: "Charlie Sierra 81, into the car park. Whether the targets are in their vehicle or not, both of you into the Little Chef. Understood?"

"Yes, yes!"

Key words were always repeated sharply. Ron's decision potentially meant that Jim and I as well as our vehicle would be deliberately compromised and therefore must remain at the rear of the convoy for the rest of the operation. A big sacrifice to make having two men down but we knew it was the right one, our targets could be meeting other associates or even changing vehicles. Or it could be a further attempt to establish whether they were being followed. Only one way to find out.

We drove into the car park and almost immediately saw the empty Sierra parked directly adjacent to the entrance. The team needed a quick update.

"From Charlie Sierra 81, target vehicle parked up, no occupants. We're going into the Little Chef, will update as soon as."

Fortunately, the car park was fairly busy and Jim was able to park the Capri out of immediate view next to the rear hedge and discreetly behind some hoarding. As we walked into the restaurant, we could see our two subjects sitting at a table by the far wall with a view of the entrance door. They looked up as we entered and watched as a waitress guided us to a table in the centre of the room. The place was about three quarters full and we were far enough from them for the hubbub of conversation to allow me to covertly transmit any necessary messages to the team outside. Jim sat with his back to the subjects; I was on the opposite side of the table with a view of our targets over his shoulder. They were soon in deep conversation and seemed to take little interest in our presence, although still keeping a watchful eye on anyone entering. They had obviously ordered a meal, so we did the same. Whilst eating, both occasionally glanced our way and it was difficult to assess if their interest was normal or whether their suspicions were aroused.

Half an hour later, their meal finished, they stood up. As if in quiet conversation with Jim, I transmitted to the team.

"Stand by, stand by, stand by! Both targets finished their meal and preparing to leave."

I could picture the instant reaction to my message in the team vehicles plotted around us over a two-mile radius; engines quickly started, music turned off, coffee chucked through windows, newspapers tossed into the back seat, adrenaline pumping, ready for the off. It was moments such as this that made mobile surveillance operations one of the most exciting areas of police work in which to be involved.

Instead of heading to the door, our two subjects went towards the toilets. We knew there was no access to the car park such as a fire door within the area they had gone to, so we remained seated and relayed what was happening to the team. A few minutes later, both men emerged from the toilet area and headed towards the till by the entrance to pay for their meal. As they passed our table one of them leaned over and hissed in my ear, "Following us, are you?"

Instinctively I said, "What are you talking about?"

This would normally have signalled a major compromise and automatically the end of our operation for the day, except that upon leaving us, these two walked over to another table and spoke quietly to its occupant, a young-looking businessman, and clearly asked him the same question. It was a crafty bit of fishing designed to put off prospective surveillance, except they blew it by confronting more than one person, confirming they didn't know who they were looking for. Jim and I stayed seated whilst they paid for their meal and left to go back to their vehicle. They both glanced back at us as they left. I got on the air.

"Stand by, stand by, stand by! Both targets out, out, out of the Little Chef and towards their vehicle. They did not, repeat not, meet anyone but they challenged us and also a member of the public so probably a fishing exercise but be alert, they are all about them. Ops Comm received?"

Ron responded. "Charlie Sierra 75 received, thanks JD, we'll go with them, you remain tail end Charlie for the foreseeable. Understood?"

"Yes, yes."

'Tail end Charlie' was the term used for the last vehicle in the convoy line. Two minutes later came the anticipated call from the convoy:

"Charlie Sierra 77 has the 'eyeball', target vehicle resuming A12 southbound, six zero miles an hour, nearside lane."

Thank heaven for that, at least they were continuing towards London and presumably hadn't been spooked. We needn't have worried, the follow continued without further problems along the A12, M25 and M11 until they eventually stopped in a public car park at Hackney in East London. There had been no more anti-surveillance moves by the pair and it seemed as though the challenge in the Little Chef had been a final act of reassurance to themselves that police were not following. Our foot team were able to watch the targets meet up with two other men in the Albion Tavern pub where they remained for an hour, deep in conversation.

Ron was in radio contact with the Met Police throughout the surveillance and they became excited when he told them of the pub meeting which turned out to be with two of their own robbery suspects. In fact, their interest was such that the Flying Squad arrived on the plot during the pub meet and it was agreed that we would hand over our side of the operation. We were, to say the least, reluctant to do that, but at the same time we knew it made absolute sense; we didn't have the resources or local knowledge to continue the job for much longer without an increased risk of compromise. So, we left the Sweeney plotted up around the Albion Tavern and returned to base for the debrief.

Some time afterwards, we learned that the arranged 'recce' of the National Westminster Bank at Hackney by our villains had indeed taken place on the day we left and shortly afterwards their plan to carry out an over-the-pavement robbery was at an advanced stage. But it seems the would-be robbers got cold feet at the last minute and the job didn't happen. Although the reason was never known to us, the rumour mill had it that the aftermath of Operation

Countryman had an effect on a number of ongoing Met operations, including this one.

Operation Countryman was a major investigation carried out by the Dorset Constabulary into corruption by the City of London and Metropolitan Police and lasted from 1978 to 1982; part of the enquiry centred around allegations that the Central Robbery Squad (still universally known as the Flying Squad) had been involved in receiving bribes from criminals in return for advanced warning of imminent police raids, arranging bail for armed robbers and fabrication of evidence. The enquiry cost between £3m and £4m and led to eight officers being prosecuted but, significantly, no convictions. The Operation Countryman findings were presented to the Home Office and the Metropolitan Police Commissioner, but despite several requests in Parliament for the Home Secretary to disclose the results, they have never been made public owing to Public Interest Immunity.

During the 1970s and 1980s, the Metropolitan Police as well as some RCS branches were involved in the running of so called 'supergrasses', professional criminals who turned Queen's evidence, usually in return for a lower sentence and subsequent protection for them and their family. My RCS branch office had responsibility for one such individual, the investigation being underway by the time I arrived on the squad. One of the two officers dealing with the prisoner/informant was overdue on his RCS secondment and as he was recalled back to his force, I was nominated as his replacement to co-handle the prisoner.

I had mixed feelings about it. On the one hand, the job would be great experience but on the other, it would be a very time-consuming operation and I would miss out on other more diverse jobs as well as the chance to develop my own work. But at the end of the day this was a unique opportunity which would probably not arise again.

Our 'supergrass', Alan 'Geordie' Lucas, was a career criminal with a penchant for armed robbery who had been arrested for committing an aggravated burglary at a mansion house in Enfield, the 'aggravated' bit relating to his possession of a loaded sawn-off shotgun. On conviction, the offence carries a maximum sentence of life imprisonment and with our man's previous history, he was looking at a lot of years inside. So, he decided to inform on his previous associates in crime and get himself a lighter sentence.

Lucas was on prison remand and the first few months of my time with him were spent, along with my partner at the time, Chris, another experienced DS, in a cell inside a segregated prison wing taking down his written statement outlining the alleged misdeeds of his former associates. The crimes he described were many and varied and on several occasions there was a necessity for him to physically show us the exact locations of where they had taken place; this of course required special permission both from the prison authority and RCS senior command.

Lucas, naturally, enjoyed his temporary 'freedom' but we found the days out quite stressful; the responsibility for his custody, security and welfare was transferred from the prison direct to us, making the whole operation to take him out incredibly resource intensive. But if we were to accurately locate the scenes of crime he was describing there was no alternative. Lucas was a very volatile character and although usually approachable, he was prone to mood swings and fits of temper if things didn't go his way. He was arrogant and blatantly revelling in his new-found status as a 'major crim'.

One of my roles in dealing with Lucas was to act as family liaison officer between him, his wife and two young daughters. Part of the terms of his Home Office status as a supergrass was an agreement that he would be allowed occasional discreet meetings with his family and so the days we took him out were useful to facilitate such encounters. The visits were strictly controlled and could only take place on certain 'approved premises' which were effectively a prison or a designated police station where his security could be ensured. The arrangement worked reasonably well and we took him out usually for one day a week to locations in Essex, Hertfordshire and Middlesex where he pointed out several exclusive properties and post offices which had been the subject of burglaries or armed robberies, some of which he admitted involvement in a 'minor' capacity and some not at all. The excursions generally ended with a visit to a pre-arranged police station where Lucas would meet up with his wife, Stella, and their two little daughters in a private secure area of the station for an hour or so. Had I known the repercussions these visits would have and the risk to my career that would ensue, they would not have taken place.

Another part of the Home Office deal was that Stella and the children would be given another identity and ensconced in a safe house in Cambridge. I was tasked with making many of the necessary arrangements which were complex and time consuming. Although Lucas and Stella originated from Newcastle, they were latterly from Neasden where their two children were born. As I was Stella's only direct secure contact with both the police and her husband – and they were both paranoid about his former partners in crime discovering where she lived – I was effectively on call 24/7. In the early days and weeks following Stella's move into the safe house, she would telephone me often, sometimes up to three or four times a day, usually in a panic over someone she thought was hanging around watching the house or a wrong number phone call she'd had, or even on one occasion being worried about the way a man had looked at her in a local shop. Her fears were understandable to a degree and particularly bearing in mind the nature of her husband's former associates, although I think she was crediting them with more ingenuity and ability than they were capable of. But I was there to keep calm waters between Lucas and Stella so that he would concentrate on supplying the evidence we required and not be distracted by concerns over the well-being of his family. So, Stella's washing machine breaking down, the hiccup over her new identity DHSS allowances not being paid, one of her daughters being bullied at the school we had got her into, etc., fell to me to resolve. On the occasions we were at the prison to resume the taking of Lucas's statement, the first hour was always taken up with giving him an account of how his wife was faring and a full description of what she'd been doing over the previous days. Necessary, but from our point of view, tedious.

There was a surprising side to Alan Lucas in that he was a first-class model maker. He described his occupation as 'unqualified chippie' but there was no doubt he had a natural talent for building small scale models of cars, planes, buildings and even people, out of virtually anything. Being a remand prisoner, he was allowed various materials in his cell and over the weeks we saw many examples of his work and there was no doubt he was good enough to have been able to earn some sort of living from it. Annoying really, I reflected, that a guy with this ability to create beautiful things had chosen instead to earn his living by causing pain and distress to innocent people. "Why would you do that?" I asked him once. He shrugged. "Easier money," was the reply.

Months later came 'D' Day. This was the culmination, the designated day when all of Lucas's information had been collated, checked for supporting evidence and a list of targets drawn up who would be simultaneously arrested and their respective addresses searched. Most of the region's RCS branch offices were involved in the round up and various police stations were earmarked to receive the prisoners. The role of Chris and myself was to remain with Lucas throughout the operation to be in a position to relay answers to any questions raised by search teams or interviewing officers.

The operation resulted in what can at best be described as average success. Many arrests were executed and a number of assorted crimes cleared up. Some convictions followed due to guilty pleas being entered, but some of the more serious offenders, notably two separate armed robbery suspects, denied everything and in the absence of corroborative evidence, were due to stand trial where Lucas's account of their involvement was to be at the heart of the prosecution cases. At least, it would have been if Lucas had not reneged on the whole deal.

He convinced himself that we had not sufficiently protected Stella or his children and that Chris and I had deliberately lied to him about her safety and well-being throughout the process. On the contrary, we had gone out of our way to ensure her safety and peace of mind; I had reacted every time to her frequent requests for assistance, often on days off or late at night and sometimes at considerable inconvenience. I told Lucas this in no uncertain terms, but he was having none of it. He told us he would take his chances at court without any help from us and therefore the arrangement was off.

Although this sudden turnaround in his attitude came as a huge disappointment, it was not entirely unexpected given his characteristic arrogance. In view of the timing of his announcement, it occurred to us that perhaps this had been his plan all along, to present us with the carrot of clearing up major crime and arresting those responsible but never intending to give evidence against them. In the meantime, he had been able to spend his remand period in comparative comfort whilst enjoying the privileges of supergrass status; the more minor criminals he had given us would then be used as collateral at his eventual sentencing. We would never know for sure whether that was his intention, but subsequent events clearly demonstrated Lucas's animosity towards the police in general, and for Chris and me in particular.

The proposed trials of his former robbery cohorts collapsed and Lucas was subsequently convicted of the aggravated burglary offence for which he had originally been arrested. He pleaded guilty and defence counsel made great play of the 'help' he had given to the police in securing the convictions of the comparatively minor offenders in our operation. He got four years but with good behaviour plus allowance for the time spent on remand, he would be released considerably sooner. The necessary 'mop up' work following the operation was carried out by the individual forces involved and we saw neither Lucas nor Stella again.

It was good to get away from reporting for duty in a prison cell for months on end and get back to normal duties; having the time and opportunity to take part in more conventional operations once again was a relief for both of us. My first 'undercover' job was just around the corner.

Chapter 10

Helping Out

Occasionally, requests were received for RCS assistance which did not involve our specialist surveillance capability. A body had been found in a Cambridgeshire wood and a post-mortem revealed he had been shot dead at close range a matter of hours prior to the discovery of the body. Information had come into the murder incident room that a certain public house in Cambridgeshire was the drinking haunt of an individual believed to have supplied the murder weapon to the killer. Nothing else was known of him other than a description; his identification was urgently needed. The request was for an undercover operation to be carried out at the pub over the next few days in an effort to identify the suspect. A colleague, Colin, and I were selected to pose as a pair of painters and decorators working locally, visiting the pub in our lunchtimes and alternate early and late evenings. Considering we had no real preparation time for the job, not to mention training, we did well under the circumstances. We acquired a beaten-up old van laden with ladders, paint and various tools and equipment to help our cover story and off we went.

There were insufficient resources to supply any form of backup and of course, being the early eighties, no mobile phones, no health and safety rules and definitely no risk assessments existed. They were all years away and thankfully, an operation under these circumstances could not happen now. Undercover officers today must pass a national selection process and an extensive training course before becoming accredited to gather intelligence and evidence.

Our first week in the pub went reasonably well, we had gradually introduced ourselves to bar staff and the locals as two freelance painters doing contract work on two sites on the edge of Cambridge. We were well-received and by the end of the week were on first name terms with the licensee and his family and even became part of the darts team! Each lunchtime and evening we kept what description we had of our potential suspect to the forefront of our minds as we had absolutely nothing else to go on, but there was no show. Fortunately for us, the pub was fairly remote and so not too busy – it was never packed which made it easier to observe everyone entering. We obviously needed to drink alcohol to maintain our story of being normal beer drinking workers, but of course we needed to bear in mind that one of us had to drive, so the plan was to take it in turns for one to drink little and the other to imbibe as a thirsty painter would do. If the suspect had not appeared by the end of the second week, the plan was to end the operation and withdraw.

Midway through week two, on an evening session, it was Colin's turn to drive, so I was the thirsty painter. Again, there had been no sign of our man, it was quite late on in the evening, and I was involved in a friendly game of darts with some locals when I realised Colin wasn't around. Assuming he'd gone to the toilet, I carried on with the game but ten minutes later, he still wasn't back so I went to the toilets to check he was OK. No sign, but returning to the bar, there he was standing at the counter looking round for me.

"Think I found him," he said, "over there."

He gestured towards a group of locals stood in the corner. Sure enough, a man wearing an army style camouflage jacket fitted the description we had.

Colin said, "Clocked him when he first came in, he's had a few and I managed to get him talking."

Colin had got even further with our suspect, who introduced himself as Steve, and said he was a member of the Territorial Army, upon which Colin commented that he'd always fancied joining the TA himself.

Their conversation resulted in our man taking Colin out to the car park where he opened the boot of his car and showed off items of military combat clothing, bits and pieces of army style equipment and, incredibly, a handgun. Colin noted the vehicle registration number and returned into the bar with the suspect, obviously inebriated, bragging to anyone who would listen about his TA experiences. We stayed in the pub for a further half hour, after which Colin bade our suspect goodnight, shook his hand and we left.

Back in the van, Colin got on the radio to the police control room and gave a pre-arranged code word and brief details of what had taken place. We parked up in a nearby gateway and waited for Steve to leave the pub. He left in his vehicle soon afterwards and we relayed his direction of travel to a waiting patrol car, resulting in him being stopped and arrested.

It turned out that Colin had correctly identified 'Steve' as the individual the murder team needed to trace and he was indeed a member of the TA. As such, he had access to an armoury and was found to be in possession of unauthorised property including two firearms and a quantity of ammunition. Although charged with those offences, he was not the man who had supplied the murder weapon. The original information had been wrong, but nevertheless we had done our bit. Or at least Colin had! He dined out on the story for some time, the emphasis, of course, being on the fact that he was on the ball and doing his duty whilst I drank beer and played darts. There were a number of episodes where those roles were very definitely reversed, but in the interests of loyalty and the protection of all parties, they are best left unpublished. And to be fair to my mate Colin, he had done a great job.

That was our last visit to the pub and our end of job report was subsequently submitted to the incident room who were more than happy with the result, though not so much with the accompanying 'incidental expenses' sheet. Our claims were eventually agreed, mainly on the basis that we had effectively been on duty for a great number of hours, largely on unpaid overtime.

Colin and I were involved in several escapades in the RCS, some repeatable, most not. One of the most memorable began early one morning in the autumn of 1984 during a surveillance operation in Hertfordshire; the job related to a meeting due to take place in London involving members of an organised crime syndicate who were in the preliminary stages of planning the movement of a huge drugs consignment to be received into the UK. The identity of one of the gang was known and he had been recently 'housed' at Hemel Hempstead. We had intelligence giving us the day of the meeting and our objective was to follow the target on leaving his home to establish the meeting location in London as well as identifying/photographing the other participants.

Following a 4.30 am briefing in the branch office, we got to our respective surveillance vehicles in the secure car park; Colin and I were in 5CS27, an Austin Princess, and with us was the branch DI, Brian. Colin was the driver with me as the front passenger and Brian in the rear seat. We were about to leave with the rest of the convoy when Brian tapped me on the shoulder and said, "JD, it's too bloody cramped in this motor, going to be a long day, think I'll go with one of the others."

He hopped out and got in the back of one of the other cars.

"He's not daft," I said to Colin, "obviously heard about your driving."

The target address being just off the M1 motorway, the team plotted around Hemel Hempstead and we drove to our designated position which was to be stationary on a grass verge running alongside the exit slip road of junction 8. It was still dark as we settled down to wait for the 'off' to be given from the pre-arranged Observation Point (OP) overlooking our target's home. It was a chilly morning, we had the engine running to keep warm and although the vehicle sidelights were on, they made little difference to what happened next.

In the wing mirror I saw a set of headlights travelling fast along the exit road towards us. The Volvo 240 suddenly veered to its nearside, mounted the grass verge and smashed into the back of us at 60 mph. The rear of our car disintegrated like a paper cup, the roof buckled and the vehicle was propelled a hundred yards forward. I don't know if it was me who held Colin's hand or whether he grabbed mine, but holding hands we were, both of us believing this was the end of the line. Our car came to a stop when it rammed into a fence and both front seats dislodged from their mountings causing Colin to be jammed against the steering wheel whilst the passenger door was flung open and my seat literally ejected sideways and forwards, slamming into the open door.

The total silence that followed was weird; we looked at each other and in those few seconds I really did not know whether I was alive or dead. Colin's sudden outburst of expletives describing the driver who had hit us was absolute sweet music – I knew Heaven wouldn't allow that sort of language.

It was nothing short of a miracle that we escaped with comparatively minor injuries. Colin suffered severe chest bruising and I had nasty cuts and abrasions to both legs with the pair of us having a degree of whiplash. But we climbed from the mangled remains of 5CS 27 and went to check on the driver of the Volvo which was still embedded in the twisted wreckage of our boot. Lady Luck was certainly smiling that day as apart from a chest impact injury and a gash on his forehead, the other driver also survived virtually intact. He was a business executive who had been partying for much of the night and fallen asleep at the wheel shortly after leaving the motorway. Local traffic police attended, the other driver was arrested for drink driving and the three of us taken to Hemel Hempstead General for treatment. The driver subsequently appeared at Hemel Hempstead Magistrates Court and was convicted for excess alcohol and dangerous driving.

Had Brian, our DI, not changed his mind about being in the back of our vehicle for the surveillance, he would probably have died that morning. Once again, those road accident gods had been in a good mood.

One afternoon, having finished an ongoing job in north London, we returned to the office for a debrief when the branch DCI called me into his office. The look on his face told me it wasn't good news.

"Sorry," he said, "I have to tell you that a Detective Chief Superintendent from another area (he named the force) has been appointed as SIO (Senior Investigating Officer) to investigate your involvement with Alan Lucas."

I stood there in disbelief.

"What the hell's going on?" I said. "What am I supposed to have done?"

"Can't discuss it JD, Chris is on leave at the moment but the two of you will be investigated and I have to serve you with the necessary Reg 7 Notice. Sorry mate."

He handed me the form and I walked out of the office in a daze. The Regulation 7 Notice related to the updated Police (Discipline) Regulations 1977 and – as with the earlier set of discipline forms for the alleged assault on the keyholder – outlined the matters under investigation.

It was said that if you went through your career without picking any Reg 7 notices up, you weren't doing your job. If that was the case, on this occasion I'd certainly hit a career high; the Reg 7 listed a total of ten allegations made by Alan Lucas concerning the occasions Chris and I had taken him out of prison to identify crime scenes and to allow him family visits. But these weren't simply disciplinary matters, the complaints consisted of allegations that we had offered him inducements to provide information about crime, allowed him to have alcohol and tobacco to which he was not entitled under prison regulations and had taken him to police stations and failed to document him properly. But the final allegation took it from frivolous to heavy:

It is alleged that you knowing Alan Lucas had received certain treatment in that he had been allowed to receive alcohol, tobacco, uncensored mail and unauthorised visits from his wife whilst being produced from Prison, conspired with others to conceal this information from the Prosecuting Authority, this information being material to the conduct of the case.

Although the allegations were currently at the disciplinary complaint level, a formal charge of criminal conspiracy could be under consideration, which I had no way of knowing. My mind went into overdrive, for a serving police officer a conviction for criminal conspiracy would not only be career ending but would probably result in imprisonment. It would be the end of the road in every conceivable respect and didn't bear thinking about. I stood outside the DCI's office reading through these crazy accusations and reflected on the loathing that Lucas must have harboured for us. Then I wondered about those who had listened to his version of events. Had they taken him seriously? Did they believe him? The fact that an outside force had been brought in to investigate suggested perhaps they did. Anger began to take over my thoughts, what the hell was I thinking, we had done nothing wrong other than perhaps failing to document every single minute of the time we spent with him – a lesson learned for the future. We had known of course that we could never completely trust the man, but these false allegations now clearly showed the depth of his animosity.

A week later, I was in a pub out in the sticks when who should walk in but my old DS from Dunstable, George Prior. We had a good old chat during which I told him about the Reg 7 notice I'd been served, and the circumstances. He said, "But you haven't been suspended?"

"No."

"No restrictions on your duties?"

"No."

"Then I would suggest the allegations aren't being treated

as seriously as they could be. I know two DCs in the Met who were served forms under very similar circumstances, both were suspended on the spot."

I was grateful for George's comments and they certainly helped my state of mind, especially as the weeks dragged on without mention from anyone in authority about what was happening with the investigation. The investigating force made no attempt to interview either of us nor even made telephone contact. It was to be months before we discovered our fate.

Part of the RCS remit was to respond where possible to assistance requests from forces within the region where additional resources were required to help out with major investigations such as murder, kidnap, blackmail or large-scale serial offending. The case of the lone criminal dubbed by the media as 'The Fox' was one of the latter. Across an area straddling Bedfordshire, Hertfordshire and Buckinghamshire over the summer of 1984, he terrorised the community by breaking into their homes at night and committing acts of rape, indecent assault and theft. He carried a shotgun and wore a home-made balaclava type hood with eye holes when committing many of the crimes, a terrifying spectacle for the victims. He was known to have a northern accent and, significantly, wore a watch on his right wrist.

Our squad was seconded to the enquiry, Operation Peanut, which was run from an incident room at Dunstable Police Station with Bedfordshire's Detective Chief Superintendent as the SIO.

We worked in pairs responding to various lines of enquiry coming into the incident room as well as routinely working night shifts when we were assigned to wait inside selected homes around The Fox's known area of operation – a rough geographical triangle around Leighton Buzzard, Dunstable and Tring. Our allocated addresses, though picked at random, fitted the profile of the type of property The Fox targeted and armed officers were also deployed to several of the more likely homes. It was a dual approach consisting of these extensive observations running alongside all the painstaking work being carried out by a large team of detectives and forensic experts.

The Fox continued to commit a horrendous catalogue of similar crimes throughout that summer, being now linked not only across the local 'triangle' but to similar offences committed in Durham and the North East. On 17th August, an offence was committed in Brampton, Yorkshire where the offender broke into the house of a couple in the early hours of the morning, tied them up at gun point and the wife was raped. The rapist cleaned himself up afterwards, cutting up part of the sheet that contained his semen and taking it with him. On leaving the premises he buried his shotgun and the stained bed linen, but both items were subsequently discovered by police. Also found were footprints, tyre tracks and small specks of yellow paint from a tree branch where the offender had reversed his car in making his getaway. Based on analysis of the paint particles, the investigation focused on tracing a 'harvest yellow' 1973–1975 Austin Allegro car of which there were believed to be around 1500 in the UK. Officers began the painstaking task of interviewing and eliminating the owners and that September, two Bedfordshire detectives went to an address in Kentish Town, London, to routinely interview one such owner.

On arrival, a man was outside the house washing his car, a yellow Austin Allegro. The officers noticed scratches on the car paintwork. The man spoke with a northern accent and wore a watch on his right wrist. Forensic analysis combined with good old-fashioned detective work had caught The Fox.

Malcolm Fairley was arrested and on 26th February 1985 he was convicted at St Albans Crown Court after pleading guilty to three rapes, two indecent assaults, three aggravated burglaries and five burglaries. He asked for a further sixty-eight offences to be taken into consideration and was sentenced to six life terms of imprisonment. There is little doubt that if police at the time had been equipped with today's advances in DNA science and digital technology, it is unlikely Fairley would have evaded arrest for as long as he did. Nevertheless, thanks to the courage of his victims, the skills of various experts and a great deal of diligent police work, he was finally brought to justice.

My three-year secondment to the RCS went far too quickly and apart from the supergrass interlude I thoroughly enjoyed my time on the squad and the frequent mobile surveillance operations and training would serve me well for the future. Most importantly, I had become a team player, learning to put my utmost trust in others and having it reciprocated. A life lesson I'm not sure I would have received anywhere else.

It was the autumn of 1985; upon leaving the Regional Crime Squad and returning to the divisional CID strength I was posted to the little market town of Leighton Buzzard. Despite its comparatively small size, it was a busy town crime wise and its DS and three DCs were kept on their toes. When I arrived on day one, my conversation with one of the divisional CID supervisors went thus:

"Just come off the crime squad then?" he asked.

"That's right," I replied.

"Lots of driving around London in fast cars and nicking major villains?"

"Only some of the time."

"Well, you're back in the real world now," said the unsmiling supervisor, "and to bring you down to earth we're putting you in charge of stolen pedal cycles."

Now I really didn't care what I would be dealing with, I was just looking forward to spending more time at home with the family and actually knowing more or less when I would be finishing work for the day, although this wasn't what I would have called a pleasant welcome. For some reason I was obviously considered too big for my boots. I had seen other officers return from squad secondments, and even from New Scotland Yard attachments, being subjected to this strange attitude of animosity on returning to division. I came to the conclusion it was their problem, not mine, and as I never discovered the underlying reason, I shrugged it off and put it down to simple jealousy.

Lesson learned: don't overly worry about what other people think.

I knuckled down to the work and began to enjoy once again the investigative process of legwork, arrest, interview, paperwork and court. Leighton Buzzard was a small and rather homely station and with the CID command situated eight miles away in Dunstable, our office was largely autonomous. We had our own typing pool, photography and fingerprint facilities, a small cell block and even the magistrates court was situated in the precincts of the station. It was a cracking work environment and I thoroughly enjoyed my time there.

One day, about three months after arriving at Leighton Buzzard, I was at Bedfordshire Police Headquarters, now situated in a much larger new building in Kempston, when I was called in to the Detective Chief Superintendent's office.

He said, "About the Lucas supergrass business, at long last we've had a result and I'm pleased to say it's good news. Had a call from the investigating force this morning and it's been resolved as no further action on any of the allegations."

A massive wave of relief surged through me. At long last.

"Those fairy tales cost me a few sleepless nights, governor, we were never even interviewed, any idea why it's taken this long?"

"They've certainly been dragging their feet," he said, "but reading between the lines, I'm guessing the whole complaint was eventually withdrawn. So go and get yourself a beer."

That was the last I heard of Alan Lucas. Well, almost. Years afterwards, I was the office manager in the Force Crime Intelligence Bureau at Headquarters when a West Midlands Crime Bulletin came across my desk; I did a double take at Lucas's photograph staring out at me. I read the details:

'At 1500 hours on Monday, 12th June 1995 an offence of Armed Robbery was committed at a Coventry post office when two males wearing balaclavas entered the sub post office each carrying a double-barrelled sawn-off shotgun. Approximately £3,000 in cash was stolen.

Wanted for this offence: Alan Lucas (alias John Dunne) and Charles Hendry (alias David Peck)'

Lucas's desire for 'easier money' hadn't left him. It doubtless never would.

One day in the autumn of 1986, I was in the Leighton Buzzard CID office when I got a phone call from the Detective Superintendent (Deputy Head of the force CID) to ask if I would be interested in an imminent vacancy on the force Drug Squad. I'd done eighteen months back in a divisional CID office and was quite enjoying the less manic work approach compared to the RCS days and I wasn't particularly looking around for a change. But secondment to specialist departments was normally via an application followed with a selection interview, a process I detested and the absence of which made me think carefully about the Superintendent's suggestion. Most of my time with the RCS had been a joy and I knew the force Drug Squad operated in a similar, though obviously more localised, fashion. They needed the vacancy filling quickly and I was given twenty-four hours to decide, so that evening Lynda and I discussed the pros and cons; we knew the hours would be longer and there would be a callout system but the office was locally based at Ampthill and it was the type of work I knew I'd enjoy. As supportive as ever, Lynda said I should go for it, so on 6th October 1986, I joined the Drug Squad.

The unit was formed in 1969 in tandem with a number of forces to combat the ever-increasing misuse of street drugs and at that time the Bedfordshire squad comprised just two officers. Dunstable Police Station was nominated as their base and when the two detectives, Rex and Dave, reported for duty on 12th August, they famously had no office, no desk, no chairs, no equipment and no real terms of reference. But it was a start, and eventually the squad was sufficiently funded to enable two DCs plus a DS for each of the main police divisions of Bedford, Luton and Dunstable.

When I joined, the squad was centralised and there were eight of us plus two DSs and an Inspector. The unit was well equipped with a number of reasonably powered vehicles and all officers were surveillance trained, albeit in-house. Following two drug awareness courses and a great deal of on-the-job learning about the methods of street dealing, drug prices and so on, I felt equipped to be, hopefully, an effective member of the squad. Nobody told me about initiation tests.

Chapter 11

Opening Doors

One of the initiation tests for a new Drug Squad officer was having to demonstrate effective use of the 'key', otherwise known as a sledgehammer, used when force was needed to gain rapid entry to somewhere, normally to recover drugs before they could be disposed of. So, it was at 6 am one morning I found myself with four other Drug Squad officers outside an apartment on the fourth floor of a block of flats on Luton's Marsh Farm estate. This was the home of Charlie Cutler, a prolific dealer, the information being that he was in possession of a large amount of amphetamines which he would be selling on later that day. Armed with a search warrant, the objective, as usual, was to gain quick access, contain the occupants and carry out a methodical search of the flat. I had the sledgehammer and my task was simply to smash the door lock – ideally with a single blow – allowing us to make a swift entry.

Taking a deep breath, I raised the 10lb 'key' with both hands and swung it over my head to give as much impetus as I could; I'd practised a few times to get the hang of the thing, but the practice session had taken place outdoors and now I was in a corridor less than two yards wide. The impetus I mentioned happened far too early and the sledgehammer continued its arc backwards out of control over my head, and with a deafening thud embedded itself in the plaster of the wall behind me. The next few minutes were pandemonium. I desperately tried to remove the 'key' from the hole as one of the 'heavies' on our unit put his shoulder to the target's door, but it refused to budge. Then the occupier of the flat opposite opened his door to find out why someone was trying to batter his wall down. Having been told who we were, he returned indoors muttering that he was going to ring the real police. By now, we'd gained entry to Charlie's flat, or to be truthful, he opened his door and asked why we hadn't knocked.

It was apparent from his attitude that he believed we wouldn't find any drugs, and indeed, the search of his flat was negative. But we were one step ahead. One of our number had been detailed to remain outside on the ground directly below the subject's flat in the event of drugs being thrown from the balcony. Sure enough, at the exact time we were trying to gain entry four floors up, in the words of our colleague, "A bag of speed fell from the sky and into my lap!" Forensic evidence linking the package to the interior of Charlie's flat and our officer's clear identification of the balcony were sufficient to convict Charlie of Possessing a Controlled Drug with Intent to Supply at Bedford Crown Court and he was sentenced to two years imprisonment. At least my 'key initiation' failure ended in a result for the Drug Squad.

But it wasn't just drugs the local residents disposed of from their balconies; coincidentally, not long after Charlie's arrest and following a brutal murder in the vicinity, one of our CID colleagues had just completed a televised interview with a BBC film crew immediately outside the same block of flats when a full sized television set exploded onto the ground thirty yards from where they were standing; it had been dropped from somewhere around the tenth floor. As the crew stood there in shock one said, "What the hell's going on with this place?"

The reply was, "Welcome to Luton."

The incident with the sledgehammer seemed to set a tone for me on the Drug Squad; whenever I was involved in anything to do with a premises forced entry, it rarely seemed to go well. We received intelligence that a half kilo of cannabis was secreted in a maisonette in Dunstable, so having acquired a Misuse of Drugs Act search warrant, five of us went to the premises early one morning armed again with our 'key'. One of the DCs was detailed to use it this time and I kept out of the way as he carefully lined it up and then swung the thing as hard as he could at the door lock. It was like Thor himself had struck the blow as the entire door crashed inwards having been parted not only from the lock mechanism but from its hinges too. I was first through the door yelling, "Police, stay where you are." Not realising in time that the door was still on its way to the ground, my leg somehow got trapped beneath it and down I went. The door became a drawbridge allowing the rest of the Drug Squad to charge over it into the flat. I scrambled up and joined in the usual chaos that accompanied a drugs raid – two were arrested and an amount of cannabis recovered. The pain in my leg escalated which wasn't surprising as an X-ray revealed it was a bone fracture just above the ankle. There followed six weeks sick leave with my leg in plaster and on my GP's suggestion I took advantage of the Police Convalescent Home facility in order to receive some quality physiotherapy whilst I had the chance.

At that time in 1991 there were two such police care centres in the UK, one at Goring-on- Thames in Berkshire and the other at Harrogate, North Yorkshire. They were started in 1890 by a lady called Catherine Gurney, who worked with the poor in London when a particular incident sparked an awareness of the special needs of police officers and their families. She found a place for an injured police officer in a convalescent home, only to find he had left early because he had been placed in a bed next to a violent criminal he had previously arrested. It struck her that specialist police-only convalescent facilities were needed and her hard work and perseverance resulted in what are now known as The Police Treatment Centres, the first in Brighton and the second being established seven years later in Harrogate. Due to capacity, the original home at Hove, near Brighton was closed and another rehabilitation centre, Flint House, opened in its place in 1988 at Goring. Catherine Gurney had devoted her life to such projects connected with the police service and her work subsequently led to the formation in 1948 of the Gurney Fund for police orphans, still in existence today as a registered charity. This amazing woman was awarded the OBE shortly before her death in 1930.

The treatment and care I received at Flint House were exceptional; the physiotherapy in particular was so beneficial I am sure it got me back on my feet a lot sooner than I otherwise would have. The food was also very worthy of mention, it was superb and I couldn't help drawing comparisons with the cuisine at Eynsham Hall years earlier, it was like a Lamborghini against a second-hand skateboard. The relaxation facilities at Goring weren't bad either, although Miss Gurney might not have approved of the thriving little bar – she was a fervent member of the Temperance Society! Whilst at Flint House, I was pleased to receive a letter wishing me a speedy recovery signed by Mr Dyer, the Chief Constable, and although perhaps a routine gesture for officers injured on duty, it indicated that senior command was aware and had taken the trouble to acknowledge my circumstances. I still have the letter.

The leg was now supporting me without too much of a problem and back at work I resolved never to be in swinging distance of the squad key ever again, but it seemed that my run of bad luck with forced entry issues wasn't quite over. Not long after my return, the squad took delivery of a newly developed hydraulically operated door opener which we had on trial having been used successfully by Merseyside Police and others. It was a complex looking thing and two of our unit went on a short course to learn how to properly operate it. The device consisted of a small suitcase-sized control box with a heavy-duty cable attached to a steel telescopic bar which was placed horizontally across the door with one end butted onto the frame. On pressing a button on the control box, the bar extended, creating extreme pressure on both sides of the frame. This left the door without side support, making it an easy task to strike it in the centre with a small handheld ram and it would swing open. We were told the device would open a locked and bolted steel door within four seconds so in theory it would remove further risk of injury or embarrassment caused by our current 'rapid entry' methods. Yeah, right.

Eager to try out the new toy, we planned to deploy it early one morning when executing a search warrant at an address situated in a particularly salubrious part of Luton. The house was a large 1930s detached residence, the occupier of which was believed to be involved in the sale and distribution of cocaine through his ownership of a company in the city. The job was at the request of Milton Keynes RCS Drugs Wing as part of a mop-up operation and it was suspected that the target, James Barker, was currently in possession of an amount of cocaine at the house. We arrived at the address at 6 am on a Friday morning along with our fully trained door opener operative, Tom, who was looking forward to getting to work with his new gizmo. It was still dark as the five of us crept up to the large brick porch at the front of the house trying not to crunch our feet too much on the gravel drive. On arrival at the porch, I thought this was going to be a real test for the equipment; the door was solid oak with huge metal studs across it. Well, in for a penny.

"Ready?" said Tom as he lined up the bar across the door a metre from the ground. He paused for a second then hit the button on the control pack. With a hardly audible hiss, the telescopic bar extended smoothly against the left side door frame and as the pressure increased, George hit the door with a small battering hammer. It worked a treat, the huge door swung open and in we charged. The telescopic bar was still in place, so George leapt over it, John and Terry dived under it and I followed Terry, crawling underneath it. Tom chose that moment to hit the other button on the control pack which released the pressure and retracted the telescopic bar. This resulted in the bar dropping to the ground, or, in this case, onto my back as I wormed my way into the drug dealer's den. No serious injury ensued, other than to pride, but I won't forget the look on James Barker's face as he tottered half asleep down the stairs in his pyjamas to be confronted by three scruffy blokes rushing towards him shouting, "Police officers, stand still!" with a fourth one (me) sprawled face down across his hallway and another cursing as he tried to de-assemble a lump of weird looking equipment. Recovering our dignity, we explained the terms of the search warrant to Mr Barker and three hours later, we completed our search of the house, finding absolutely nothing. As we discussed at the later debrief, it hadn't been a complete waste of time because we now knew how not to deploy a hydraulic door opener.

A great deal of drugs intelligence was generated by the use of registered informants, the control and management of which required training and much careful handling. This was particularly the case with the Drug Squad as many of the informants themselves were addicts whose lives simply revolved around acquiring the next fix and if that necessitated stealing money from their family, committing crime or 'grassing up' anybody at all, then so be it. It was alarming to see the depths to which they would go, the people they would hurt and the lying and cheating that was a normal part of their everyday existence. A number of them managed to avoid imprisonment and were helped into the rehabilitation process but I have to say hand on heart that in almost seven years on the squad, sadly, I was not aware of a single completely successful rehab case.

Nationally, the strategy of drugs investigation was demonstrated by an inverted triangle: local Drug Squads were at the bottom point of the triangle with Regional Drugs Wings (RCS offshoots) in the centre and the upper tier being a combination of the newly formed National Drugs Intelligence Unit (NDIU) and HM Customs & Excise (HMCE). The theory was that at whatever level drug supplying existed, there was a dedicated resource to deal with it from street level to organised importation.

When I joined the Drug Squad in 1986, the UK was in the midst of a rapidly spreading heroin 'epidemic' across its major cities and towns and although cannabis and

138

amphetamine dealing remained a perpetual problem, our focus was on identifying and taking out the heroin suppliers.

One evening I received information from an informant we'll call 'J' about heroin dealing taking place from a house in Luton; the dealer was from out of town and had effectively commandeered the house on a temporary basis to sell his drugs. J, although an addict, had provided previously reliable intelligence resulting in a conviction at court. We mounted an operation to try to verify the information by setting up carefully planned observations on the house which was something of a 'squat'. J had identified the dealer as one Billy Owens; he had a record, so we had photographs and a good description. We managed to acquire an Observation Point (OP) from the upstairs office of some disused premises almost opposite our target address.

The information was that the dealing was taking place during the early evening on Thursdays and Fridays, so the plan was that if individuals were seen to enter the address and leave again minutes afterwards, we would have a covert reception committee nearby to take them off the street and recover any drugs they may have scored from the dealer. The following Thursday, I was in the OP from early afternoon in the hope of identifying Owens and any vehicle he might arrive in. There was no sign of him but around 5 pm I saw one of our local addicts knock on the door, go inside and hurriedly leave two minutes afterwards. I'd hardly given the radio instruction to arrest the addict as soon as he was out of sight of the address than a second one knocked on the door and was swiftly admitted. Again, he left shortly afterwards and a few minutes later I received confirmation over the radio that both 'customers' were in custody with a positive result, in other words, both in possession of drugs.

A conviction for an offence of possessing with intent to supply often relies on the circumstances but it is crucial that the amount of the drug in the defendant's possession is sufficient to indicate that it could not reasonably have been for personal use. So once having evidence of dealing (we had two drug users already in custody in possession of heroin having just left the address) it made sense to swiftly hit the squat and recover as much of the drug as we could and arrest Owens or whoever was dealing. The decision was made.

"All units, Strike! Strike!" I shouted over the radio. It was very frustrating having to remain in situ and watch the raid go down without being involved, but OP security was paramount and I would have to wait until it was safe to leave without being observed. The squad strike team, armed with search warrant and a 'key' went through the door within a minute of my call, the back entrance being covered by two DCs to head off any escape attempt. They found Owens in a ground floor back room along with a 'minder' plus another local addict who was sitting in a corner of the room smoking a joint. On the floor where they had been hurriedly thrown from a small table when the door crashed in were several wraps of street heroin; some had spilled onto the threadbare carpet as if someone had been shaking a pepper pot around. The surprise element had worked well on this occasion, and although Owens and his mate vociferously denied ownership of the drugs, saying it was down to the unfortunate guy in the corner with the joint, none of them resisted arrest and a total of almost two ounces of heroin was recovered with a street value of some £2,000. Owens' vehicle was found parked two streets away and a coded dealing list recovered from the glove box.

In interview, the two customers both said they had scored the heroin from a guy they only knew as 'Greaser' at the squat; Owens' criminal intelligence record showed he was known as Greaser. He was subsequently charged with Possessing a Class A Controlled Drug with intent to supply. He pleaded not guilty at his trial at Bedford Crown Court and part of the defence ploy was to play 'hunt the informant'. In those days, material the prosecution was not going to use was only made available to the defence if it was considered relevant. Sensitive material could be withheld and that decision was made by the prosecution, not the court. So, quite correctly, the fact that the original information was given by J was not disclosed.

During the trial, a defence allegation was that Owens had been 'set up' by someone with a grudge who had tipped off the police. I was in the witness box under cross-examination from defence counsel:

"Officer, you were in charge of this police operation, were you not?"

It always bugged me that many barristers had this condescending and sarcastic turn of phrase when examining witnesses, the majority of whom, after all, were there to simply tell the court the truth about what they knew. It was normal practice for police officers to be put through the mill of course, we were used to it, but I worried about the justification of publicly criticising, and often humiliating, victims of crime as well as honest members of the public. And this particular advocate was swaggeringly good at it.

"Yes, I was," I replied.

"So, what made you decide to set the operation up in the first place?"

"Information received."

"Where from?" The crunch question.

"A reliable source."

"And who or what was that reliable source?"

"I'm sorry, I can't say any more than that."

Mr Swagger held the lapels of his gown, leaned slightly backwards and with a half-smile on his face turned towards the jury and then slowly swayed back to me, pausing for effect.

"And why pray, is that, officer?"

"I cannot reveal the source in open court."

At this point, the judge intervened.

"Officer, are your superior officers aware of the identity of this source?"

"Yes, your honour."

"And who is the most senior detective officer in Bedfordshire?"

I gave the name of the Detective Chief Superintendent.

"Very well officer," said the judge. "I would like him in this court at ten o'clock tomorrow morning."

Bloody hell, this was getting seriously out of hand, it should have been a straightforward trial: defence asks for informant's identity, prosecution declines on the grounds of public interest, the judge rules in our favour and the trial continues. This was not in the game plan but of course the judge is king of his court and what he says goes. The court was adjourned and in the corridor outside, the prosecuting counsel told me the judge had got out of bed the wrong side, which wasn't particularly helpful.

Apprehensively, I hotfooted to Bedfordshire Police Headquarters to seek an urgent audience with the DCS. Fortunately, he was in his office when I got there.

"Governor," I began, "I'm involved in a trial at St Albans Crown Court, are you free tomorrow morning?"

He guessed what was coming. "Tell me everything," he said, "including anything the court doesn't know about." Ten minutes later, he knew the lot. "And you've been directed to disclose the informant in open court?"

"Yes sir."

"OK, he said, "don't worry, I'll see you there in the morning."

What a weight off my shoulders to hear him say that. I knew we would lose a case rather than disclose the identity of an informant under these circumstances but it was still a huge relief knowing that if and when that happened, the squad would have the backing of the Detective Chief Superintendent.

I arrived at court the following morning at 9.30 am sharp so I could brief the prosecuting counsel that the DCS would be attending. The rest of the Drug Squad who were due to give evidence were in a separate room as I could not have contact with them due to being partway through my own evidence. Ten am came and no sign of the boss. Time to worry. Ten fifteen, our case is called and the DCS is nowhere to be seen. I was called back into the witness box for the resumption of my cross-examination by Mr Swagger.

"Officer, having received this information allegedly relating to the defendant, what did you do with it?"

Mr Swagger was definitely not swaggering as much. What's going on, I thought, why is he no longer playing hunt the informant?

"I made enquiries to verify the accused's identity and that of the address he was using."

"And then what?"

The informant line of questioning had obviously been dropped and more surprisingly, with no intervention from the judge. My cross-examination continued for another half an hour but with the kind of questioning to be expected. The trial ran its course and Owens was eventually convicted on a unanimous verdict and sentenced to eighteen months' imprisonment. But what had happened to change the judge's mind and consequently the defence's line of questioning? I discovered part of the answer from what the prosecuting barrister told me. It seems the DCS had arrived at court and gone directly to the judge's chambers which is why I hadn't seen him. The two of them were in discussion for twenty minutes resulting in the judge summoning both counsel to his chambers and directing Mr Swagger to discontinue his line of questioning towards me. To this day I have no idea what was said during those twenty minutes, although a few days later I did bump into the DCS at Headquarters, and asked him. He smiled and said, "Don't worry about it, all resolved." Respect.

Chapter 12

Ode to Heroin

One of the early jobs I was lucky enough to be involved with on the Drug Squad concerned an increasing amount of intelligence the unit had received relating to the large scale dealing of heroin, mainly in the Luton area. Much of the information was from a sensitive local source successfully cultivated by my predecessor on the squad who had deservedly been promoted and, as was the system, posted elsewhere. The investigation had produced a lead in the Netherlands which it had been decided would be followed up by Bedfordshire officers in order to ensure the protection of our interests. So, along with my DS, Tony, off I went to Amsterdam. Whatever could be said of the Dutch Police, especially their Drug Squad officers, they will never be accused of not being hospitable. We were met at Schiphol airport and whisked off to their office in central Amsterdam for a 'briefing'. A couple of hours and several very large glasses of briefing later, they dropped us at our hotel somewhere in the Netherlands. I will confess to not recalling a great deal of the remainder of the evening and neither could Tony; well, it had been a long day and we were tired...

The following morning, feeling as fresh as two dead daisies, we had to attend a briefing (a proper one this time) with the Drugs Liaison Officer (DLO), a Metropolitan Police DCI, at the British Embassy in The Hague, where we were to explain the detail of the UK side of the enquiry and establish some formal lines of communication. Despite our thumping heads, we found The Hague a hugely impressive area and it was a shame we had little time to explore. At the Embassy, we were ushered into a large wood-panelled office on the second floor where the DLO sat behind a huge oak desk.

"Good morning gentlemen," he said, "please take a seat."

We sat down in front of the desk and Tony placed his briefcase on the corner of the desk next to the DLO's own briefcase. We chatted in general terms about the enquiry, and Tony announced that we had some new intelligence to discuss. Reaching to pick up his briefcase, he grabbed the wrong one and swung it, like you do, towards himself and all would have been well had its lid stayed fastened. As it was, the case snapped open and disgorged its contents, partly onto the desk but mainly across the floor. Never have I seen so much paper scattered over such a small area and I imagine, neither had the DLO. We couldn't see his face as we scrabbled about on our knees under the desk desperately picking up bits of paper, though we did catch a large sigh and an unmistakeable, "Jesus!" coming from above. The next few minutes spent crawling about did nothing for our hangovers and even less for the DLO's patience.

"Right, let's get on with this," he snapped, and his tone suggested we really should hurry up, so we lurched back into our chairs. At least, Tony did. I came up so quickly I cracked my head on the underside of the huge oak desk which made my headache ten times worse and increased an existing desire to slink away and be sick in a corner. The scenario would have resembled a clip from a *Pink Panther* film, the only missing ingredient being a small Chinese gentleman leaping from a wardrobe and attacking us.

When we eventually sat down again, our host's papers having been stuffed back into his briefcase, he leaned forward and suggested we 'go away' (I think those were the words he used) and get a bucket of coffee down us before returning to finish our meeting later in the day. Being fairly sound advice, that's what we did, even though it meant going in the wrong direction on the tram system (which we didn't realise we needed to buy a ticket for BEFORE getting on) and which made us late for round two of our summit with the DLO at the Embassy. Thank goodness he was a (fairly) forgiving man and as the meeting progressed, we began to feel better and, subsequently, with the DLO's help, we actually formed a strategy for our job in the UK.

It was a successful trip and only unfortunate that neither of us could accurately recall every detail of the beginning or indeed the end of the two-day visit as the Amsterdam Drug Squad swung into action on the hospitality front yet again on our final night. It was a very good evening involving food, drink and music plus there were a couple of incidents, the first of which will remain forever unexplained. Halfway through the festivities, a group of Benedictine monks came into the bar. We guessed they weren't there for a stag night or a promotion do, and they simply stood there looking around at us in a sort of, well, monkish way, and then trooped out again. You could be forgiven for thinking it was the beginning of one of those jokes, 'A group of monks walk into a bar in Amsterdam…' but it really did happen. We just wished we knew why.

The second happening that night concerned a Channel 4 TV crew in the bar who were en route to Germany for the making of a TV documentary. One of the female reporters had a brown coat almost exactly the same as the one I had, and on leaving, she mistakenly picked up mine and cleared off with it and her crew to Germany. I hadn't realised what had happened until it came time to leave and I put her coat on. Being a detective, I realised that something was wrong and it was confirmed when Tony gleefully pointed out that the sleeves finished halfway between my elbow and wrist. The sequel was that, having contacted Channel 4 in London, incredibly, a month later, I went down to their studios and managed to retrieve my much-travelled coat!

One of the most effective aids to many forms of policing is the use of specially trained dogs, the breed usually depending on the job to be done. You will recall the encounter with Zimba, my German Shepherd dog in shining armour earlier – he was classed a General Purpose Dog (GPD) and they work with human scent, being used for searching and tracking as well as chasing fleeing suspects and holding them until the handler can make the arrest. A number of other breeds are used by forces including Dobermans, Rottweilers and Labradors but one of the most effective I ever saw was a little Springer Spaniel called Poppy. We didn't have a drugs dog attached to the unit but nine times out of ten when going out on a drugs 'raid' we enlisted the assistance of Poppy and her human, Tony. Poppy loved her drugs work and finding a stash of well-concealed narcotics made her day almost as much as it made ours! The squad had many successful drug recoveries and arrests due to her nose, from cannabis and amphetamines to heroin and crack cocaine.

A dog's sense of smell is two thousand times stronger than that of a human and fifty times more sensitive; I was always intrigued watching Poppy work; nose down and guided by Tony, she would charge about all over a room or vehicle with seemingly no purpose, and then stop suddenly. If positive, her little tail would become a blur like a mini circular fan and she'd start to paw and dig at the spot, which was when we knew we were generally onto a winner.

One day, we were preparing to execute a Misuse of Drugs Act warrant to search for heroin at a house in Luton; we'd had the briefing, along with Poppy and Tony, and were about to leave the police station to go to the address. I was sat behind the wheel of one of the squad cars with the driver's door open when for some reason Poppy hurtled across the yard and leapt onto my lap – she was so fast I didn't even realise it was her at first; but I was aware of excruciating pain in my nether regions where she landed. I yelled in agony which scared the poor dog half to death; she leapt off my lap and back across the yard to Tony, who could hardly stand for laughing. Then I became aware of a warm wet sensation spreading across the groin area of my jeans, and this time I knew it wasn't me.

If the dog became too excited or stressed, she would promptly relieve herself. Thanks Poppy, with no time to change, I had to remain in my jeans whilst we executed the warrant at Luton. But maybe it brought us luck because Poppy found almost an ounce of heroin concealed in a mattress, and guess what, she was so chuffed she finished off what she'd started on my jeans, this time over a duvet... the occupier was very unhappy about his wet bedding and even unhappier when he was remanded in custody charged with Possessing Diamorphine (heroin) with Intent to Supply. Like all the drugs dogs and despite her incontinence, little Poppy was absolutely worth her weight in gold, bless her.

One of the Drug Squad's problems at the time was that we were the only mobile surveillance capability available to the force, and on occasions our services were required to assist in crime enquiries that were sometimes difficult to resolve by conventional methods. But one particular armed robbery investigation was an unusual example. The offence had been committed at a jewellers' shop in the town and the offender had been identified and 'housed'. A surveillance team was required to plot the area and provide sufficient resources to monitor the suspect when he was on the move and arrest him.

Half a dozen of us were in the back of an unmarked van and despite being well wrapped in heavy windcheaters, scarves and woolly hats, it was bitingly cold. Not surprising really, it was 6.30 am on a dark January morning and the damn heater didn't work. It was uncharacteristically quiet in the van, none of the usual banter you'd expect, but on this occasion we had to adhere to strict radio silence so every movement of our target could be accurately relayed from one of the OPs without interruption, allowing us to be in precisely the right spot at the right moment for when the arrest strike was called.

The need for such precision was paramount as our target was a man dubbed by the prison service 'the most violent prisoner in Britain', one Michael Peterson aka Charles Bronson, and a man who would most definitely not surrender. Released from Gartree prison just two months earlier in October 1987, he had originally been sentenced to seven years' imprisonment for armed robbery in 1974, but owing to a catalogue of extreme violent crimes committed

148

whilst inside, he received a number of additional consecutive sentences, spending many months in solitary confinement. This resulted in numerous transfers from prison to prison during which he spent time in all of England's three high security psychiatric hospitals: Broadmoor, Rampton and Ashworth. A large and extremely fit, very dangerous individual whose proposed arrest had required careful planning to avoid the possibility of injury to anyone. Especially us.

The RCS had been approached to do the job but were committed on an ongoing kidnap operation in Essex.

The van moved quickly through Luton's Marsh Farm estate and quietly came to a halt just out of sight of Five Springs, one of the three blocks of fifteen-storey flats on the estate, and where Bronson was living. We had officers in two OPs with 'eyes' on both exit doors to Five Springs. The intelligence was that every morning between 7 and 7.30 am Bronson would go for a jog around the estate whilst still dark, returning to his flat half an hour later. Our basic plan was to arrest him in mid-jog, put him into the van and take him into custody. Knowing he would be unlikely to agree with our plan, we needed some form of inducement strategy and so it was that one of the squad's fittest and strongest detectives, Pete, became our designated 'persuader'. The idea was that Pete would walk towards Bronson as if on a morning stroll to work and with the element of surprise, once level, would tackle him with sufficient force that Bronson would be temporarily off guard; at that moment the van would draw up and the rest of us brave officers would pile out, handcuff him and put him in the van.

Sure enough, at 7.05 am, the radio crackled away in the van: "Stand by, stand by, target out, out of the rear exit of Five Springs, wearing a dark tracksuit and running slowly in the direction of the front of the block. He's out of my sight, OP 2, over to you."

"OP 2 has visual, confirm target wearing dark tracksuit and light-coloured trainers, he's running across the grass area in the direction of Wauluds Bank Drive, 62 alpha receiving?"

Pete responded, "62 alpha, yes, yes, getting into position."

We were on the move in the van heading along Wauluds Bank Drive; we could make out Bronson jogging towards us and becoming clearer in the street lighting as he got closer. Nick was riding shotgun in the van and updated the team with our position: "Five zero has visual, we're in position. Ready when you are, 62 alpha."

"62 alpha, yes, yes."

Peering through the windows, we could see Pete some fifty yards in front of us casually walking across the grass towards Bronson, who was shadow boxing as he jogged, seemingly oblivious to anyone else. As they levelled, we could see a brief exchange of words between them, then from nowhere Pete unleashed a right hook that connected with Bronson's chin and felled him like a sack of bricks. Bronson dropped to his knees and although clearly shaken, struggled back to his feet before Pete hit him once again. We shot across the grass in the van and screeched to a halt beside a mercifully disorientated Bronson who was still attempting to get up; we leapt on him and began the difficult process of putting handcuffs on his wrists and ankles. It was like dealing with squirming concrete, but we eventually managed to lift him bodily onto the floor of the van, and despite his manacles and half a dozen of us sitting on him he continued to struggle violently, all the while screaming obscenities. On the way to the station, he twisted and struggled and it took all of us to restrain him; I knelt on one of his arms in an effort to stop him thrashing around – he flexed his bicep muscle and physically lifted me!

At the police station, once he had calmed down, Bronson was interviewed about the jewellery robbery by Andy and Dave, two detectives from Luton CID. Throughout the interview, he insisted on dropping to the floor and performing one-handed press ups and on being requested to sign the interview notes, he tore them up. The histrionics didn't help him though, he was subsequently convicted of the robbery and returned into the prison system for a further four years. For the time being at least, he was no longer a danger to the public.

As I mentioned earlier, during that period of the late eighties, the focus of Drug Squads tended to be concentrated on the targeting of heroin dealers and although many of the small-time operatives were addicts themselves, there was a significant number who were not. These individuals were making good money from peddling the drug, often 'cutting' it with   other substances such as sugar, talcum powder or baking soda so they could sell more at a lesser expense to themselves. I knew of one particular lowlife who cut his heroin wraps with brick dust before selling them on.

A dealer who came to our notice over a period of months was a keep-fit fanatic called Tim Christie; he lived in Northamptonshire but operated from various addresses across Hertfordshire and Bedfordshire and was making a small fortune supplying quantities of heroin to a network of smaller dealers. He changed vehicles, routes and addresses regularly, was 'surveillance conscious' and worked alone.

We began an intelligence gathering operation to try to pinpoint the optimum time and place to hit Christie in possession of the maximum amount of heroin. We were having more and more requests for our surveillance ability and of course such diversions inevitably led to a depletion of our drugs work as the deployment of a full team usually required the squad's entire strength for the extent of the operation. A surveillance capability is an extremely expensive resource leading of course to budgetary implications, which in turn led to political considerations, i.e., 'our job is more in the public interest than yours' etc.

So, the problem with the Christie job was that we had a number of simultaneous operations running and it was difficult to devote sufficient intelligence gathering time to investigating his movements. Trying to keep all the plates spinning, we opted to select a day when the intelligence suggested Christie was most likely to be in possession of a reasonable quantity of heroin and execute a search warrant. He was subsequently housed at a flat above a shop in Luton and a warrant obtained. Again, owing to the nature of the substance we were searching for, rapid forced entry was required. So, at 8 am on a Saturday morning, in went Christie's door courtesy of our hydraulic key (which we were now more adept at operating) and we charged through the gap into his flat, the DS in charge shouting the usual, "Police officers, stand still, we have a search warrant!"

We were used to confronting a variety of receptions on these occasions, but I must admit this one did take us aback; Christie was stood in the small hallway, naked to the waist, face contorted with anger and screaming that he would burn us alive, which is when we saw he was holding a lit blowtorch. The DS and I were nearest to him and as he lurched towards us we rushed him together, managing to take him down on his back; fortunately for us, he lost his grip on the blowtorch and it landed just inside the kitchen on the bedding of a dog basket which promptly went up in flames. Fortunately, the dog – a terrier ironically called 'Lucky' – wasn't in bed at the time as he was busy watching his master grappling with the Drug Squad but on seeing his blankets suddenly ablaze, he took fright and exited the flat via the hole where the front door had been. Christie screamed, "You w......s, he never goes out without a lead, he'll never come back now!"

Whilst three of us were struggling to restrain a still violent Christie on the hall floor, the other two DCs were committed to trying to stamp out the fire in the basket which had now ignited the kitchen wallpaper although George solved that immediate problem by chucking a washing up bowl of water over everything. Taking into account the broken door, a fire ravaged dog basket and kitchen wall, as well as his drenched floor and the missing dog, I suppose Christie's displeasure was understandable. But we had a job to do, and he wasn't helping us do it, so once we had him overpowered and handcuffed, we were able to search the flat for his heroin supply. Unfortunately, there wasn't one. All we found on that occasion was a small amount of cannabis resin for his personal use. The result was a shame, although Christie did get his comeuppance some time afterwards at Bedford Crown Court where, as a result of another operation, he was convicted for possessing heroin with intent to supply and sentenced to three years. Anyway, the day we visited his flat wasn't a complete disaster for him: Lucky wandered back in as we were leaving.

The world of heroin addiction is a miserable and never-ending cycle of arranging the next fix. From interviewing many addicts – I don't like the term 'junkies' – it seems they never achieve the level of their very first 'high' but that doesn't stop them trying. One of the first addicts I met was twenty-five-year-old Terry Francis who was in the accident and emergency department of the Luton and Dunstable Hospital where he had been taken following a suspected heroin overdose. Prior to being discharged, he became talkative and according to him, he'd injected the 'usual amount' but the purity of the drug was apparently greater than normal, allegedly resulting in the overdose. He was in a depressed state and said how much he wanted to get clean even though he'd already had two attempts at rehabilitation. At one point he fished a crumpled piece of notepaper from his pocket which he showed to me: it was a poem written in scrawled untidy handwriting describing heroin addiction. He said he didn't know who'd written it but that it described his world better than he could himself. The poem was quite evocative and although not a masterpiece of verse, was undoubtedly penned by someone with a profound knowledge of the dark hopelessness of addiction.

Take Me In Your Arms

So now, my friend, you've grown tired of grass,
LSD, speed, cocaine and hash,
and someone, pretending to be a true friend,
said, 'I'll introduce you to Miss Heroin.'

Well darling, before you start fooling with me,
just let me instruct you as to how it will be.

I will seduce you and make you my slave,
I've sent men stronger than you to their grave.
You think you could never become a disgrace,
and end up addicted to poppy seed waste.

You'll start to inhale me one afternoon,
and you'll take me in your arms very soon.
And once I've entered deep in your vein,
the craving will drive you nearly insane.

You'll swindle your mother out of all she has saved.
You'll turn into something vile and depraved.
You'll mug and you'll steal for my narcotic charm,
and only feel contentment when I'm in your arms.

The day when you realize the monster you've grown,
you'll solemnly swear to leave me alone.
If you think you've got that mystical knack,
then sweetie, just try getting me off your back.

The vomit, the cramps, your gut tied in a knot,
the jangling nerves screaming for one more shot.
The hot chills and cold sweats, withdrawal pains,
can only be saved by my little white grains.

There's no other way, and no need to look,
for deep down inside you'll know you are hooked.
You'll desperately run to the dealers and then,
you'll welcome me back to your arms once again.

And when you return just as foretold,
I know that you'll give me your body and soul.
You'll give up your morals, your conscience, your heart.
And you will be mine, till Death Us Do Part.

Terry told me he copied it from an article in a rock music magazine; it seems he showed it to anyone who'd listen in an effort to explain what he was going through. Over the years, there have been variations of the poem circulating across the internet along with many claims of authorship, none verified.

I got to know Terry well during my time on the Drug Squad – he was an only child and still lived with his parents in a smart detached home in a pleasant residential area. His mum and dad were at their wits end with the progressive nightmare of their son's addiction; his father told me it was like living with two different people and never knowing which one they would be dealing with. One was a sick, pale shadow of their boy, but still their boy, the other was a sullen and disruptive individual with violent mood swings. Terry went into rehabilitation on a number of occasions following our first meeting at the hospital, and each time all went well for several weeks, sometimes months, but ultimately, he would always re-engage with former addict friends or they would find him, and over the next few years the cycle continued.

One day, I was driving along Old Bedford Road in Luton with a colleague when we saw Terry walking along the pavement. Although he had come out of rehab a month or so earlier, his father had said he believed Terry was already back on the 'gear' and indeed was dealing heroin to fund his habit, so this had to be treated as a stop and search under the Misuse of Drugs Act. As soon as we pulled up alongside him, he ran off down the road. We leapt from the car, chased after him and a hundred yards further on, between us, brought him down onto the pavement, but not quick enough to prevent him stuffing a quantity of heroin powder into his mouth. We forced him to spit some of it out but he swallowed a considerable amount, not necessarily a life-threatening quantity but clearly sufficient to warrant immediate medical attention. So, it was déjà vu back at the hospital.

This time he wouldn't speak to us which wasn't surprising, he'd obviously just 'scored' from a dealer and had tried to dispose of the evidence by swallowing it, thereby attempting to avoid a charge of possessing with intent to supply. What a state of mind, we reflected, to be willing to risk your life for the sake of £300 worth of street heroin. Unfortunately for him, the amount we recovered from his pockets was sufficient to prove it was too excessive a quantity for personal use and at St Albans Crown Court he was subsequently convicted of possessing with intent to supply. Through a combination of support from social services and a dedicated probation officer, Terry was lucky to be given a suspended sentence and ordered by the judge to embark on an intensive rehabilitation programme. I never saw him again and his parents moved out of the area so I lost contact with the family. I hope he came through it all, even though the statistics sadly suggest otherwise.

Sometimes on a straightforward search warrant execution we would need to employ a degree of subterfuge to gain access to the address, usually because the occupier was known to us and was aware of our normal tactics, i.e., if our knock at the door wasn't immediately answered, it would be followed by a rapid entry of one sort or another, often accompanied by some unavoidable collateral damage. The type of drug we were after also had a bearing on our methods of entry: a block of cannabis resin is more difficult to quickly dispose of than a bag of powder for example, so where we knew there would be some difficulty in getting into a premises and we were looking for heroin, cocaine or amphetamine powder, then we needed a cunning plan to allow us to get in as fast as possible. To that end, we had an array of uniforms we could call upon, ranging from that of a paramedic to a GPO engineer, depending on expediency, circumstances and the location. The aim was to get the occupier to unlock the door and open it, if only by a fraction. Then we were in.

One of the most successful of the fancy dress ploys was the postman's uniform. I used it myself a few times and regardless of the drugs result, we usually managed to get rapidly through the door, although on one occasion it did take a tad longer. The address was a fifth-floor flat in Hockwell Ring, Luton and the object was to gain entry and locate, according to the intelligence, 'several ounces' of street amphetamine powder. We knew the dealer as one Derry Crossman and that the door to his flat would be bolted, possibly barricaded and may even have a reinforced inner shell. Our hydraulic door opener would have worked but it was broken! There was a spyhole in the door for the occupier to identify callers, which, if we did our job right, should work to our advantage. Time for my Postman Pat alter ego.

It was 8 am and although there were a few people about around Hockwell Ring, no one took any notice as we entered the lift in pairs so as not to attract too much attention. It was all quiet on the fifth floor as we met up at the end of the corridor. The simple plan was that two members of the squad would be either side of the target door out of the spyhole eyeline with me in full view wearing my coat, cap and bag as the postie. We knew Crossman to be potentially violent and we had no intelligence as to who else, if anyone, was in the flat with him. I knocked on the door and waited ten seconds or so: no sound, nothing. I knocked again, harder. This time I could hear movement, then a muffled deep voice growled, "Who is it?"

"Post."

"At this time? Bit f…… early, aren't you?"

"Not ordinary mail, Special Delivery, someone's paid a lot of postage."

"Well put it through the f…… letter box."

"Sorry sir, can't, it's quite a large parcel."

"Who's it for?"

"D. Crossman."

"For f…. sake, leave it on the doorstep then."

This was dragging on too long so I adopted my exasperated voice:

"Look sir, I'm not allowed to leave it, I need a signature and I haven't got time to argue so if you won't sign for it I'm taking it back to the sorting office and you'll have to come in and collect it."

All went quiet and knowing that Crossman would be carefully watching me through his spyhole, I looked angry and adjusted the post office bag on my shoulder as if preparing to leave. "OK, up to you," I called. "You'll have to collect it from down town."

As I began to move away from the door, I heard the click of a bolt drawn back followed by another. The sound of a key being turned came from within and the door slowly opened an inch or so. Yes! I was still nearest the door and we had to make use of every second of it being ajar so I charged forward as hard as I could; my shoulder hit the door which flew open and knocked Crossman off balance. This was down to the element of surprise and nothing to do with power or strength on my part, I was a skinny 11.5 stone individual, albeit a determined one. The lads piled in to the flat with our man having no time to react, other than screaming, "You f..... bastard!" at me as two of the DCs pinned him to the floor. He was told who we were, as if he didn't know, and shown the search warrant. A quick check of the place revealed there were no other occupants and we began the search. Crossman became more and more abusive and wound himself up to the point of striking out and despite being handcuffed, hit one of my colleagues full in the face. We swiftly restrained him and he was arrested for assault on police. Double handcuffed to a radiator, he continued to rant and rave whilst we carried out the search of his flat; it took about twenty minutes to find what we were looking for: five ounces of 15 per cent pure pink amphetamine sulphate in a small plastic bag, carefully taped to the underside of the toilet cistern cover.

Drugs are no different to other commodities in terms of buying and selling, the more you buy in bulk the cheaper it is and the greater the profit, particularly when you dilute it with a 'cutting' agent such as glucose or baking powder.

Depending on the local market, an ounce of amphetamine would have cost perhaps £70 and sold on in one-gram deals at £5 each, an ounce would net around £140, and if cut, would make even more. Crossman's hoard was worth a potential minimum of £700 to him with an outlay of half that amount. Not a bad profit margin. He pleaded guilty to the dealing offence and in view of his history, went to prison for twelve months.

Chapter 13

Gigs and Raves

Occasionally, a pleasant diversion from our usual work came along during my time with the Drug Squad: the first was a request from Dunstable Division that we attend an open-air concert held in the grounds of Woburn Abbey in July 1990, starring rock singer Tina Turner. The idea was that we mingle with the crowd in an effort to spot any suspected drug dealing. We could have told the bosses that the probability of widespread drug deals going down at a Tina Turner gig were not too likely and the chances of spotting any that did were even more remote, but hey, who were we to argue? Bit of a job to detect illegal drug use amongst 60,000 punters but we did our best! The only 'professional' success, if you could call it that, was giving a caution to two bohemian 'free spirited' middle-aged ladies openly sharing a marijuana spliff between them whilst swaying to Tina's 'Simply the Best'. Anyone could have been forgiven for thinking they were watching a scene from *Absolutely Fabulous* as the pair of them continually fell over each other in fits of giggles. The concert was Tina Turner's Farewell Tour across Europe; it was excellent and although not particularly a fan at the time, I was converted. So much so, I bought her album of the tour the following week!

For some reason, we were again asked to attend the next Woburn concert, this time featuring the rock group, Dire Straits. It was another great show with yet a further Drug Squad 'success'. Well, sort of. A fight broke out between some teenage lads, resulting in their arrest by our uniform colleagues and being escorted to the police holding area marquee. I say marquee, more a six-man camping tent. One of the miscreants was found to have a small bag of Ritalin tablets stuffed down his sock, so we were called. Ritalin being a stimulant and a class B controlled substance under the Misuse of Drugs Act, he was arrested on suspicion of possessing with intent to supply and taken off to the police station for processing. Not a Pablo Escobar moment, but at least it gave some support to the perhaps tenuous reason for our attendance at the gig. Anyway, it was a damn good day out.

Just prior to the Dire Straits concert, owing to a sudden vacancy on our unit I had actually been promoted to DS, which had come as something of a shock, not least because the accepted protocol in the service was that promotion from any specialist department always resulted in a uniform posting. This was consistently a sticking point for me because, regardless of rank, I always wanted to remain generally in the field of dedicated crime investigation. I had been assured on a number of occasions that the time spent in uniform on general duties in the higher rank would usually be no longer than two years when one could then apply for whatever post was available at the time. But there was never a guarantee and I saw several officers promoted from a specialist department that they enjoyed into a uniform role as a Sergeant or Inspector, and there they remained. Of course, many pursuing a career path were eager for promotion and indeed, some of them made excellent senior officers. The most successful strategy to remain where one wanted to be – notwithstanding the later thorny issue of tenure – was to stay in the rank of Constable, which I had been more than happy to do, but I'd had to qualify to Sergeant to get into the CID in the first place and it was subsequently made pretty clear that I should complete the process and go through the interview and assessment procedure. Reluctantly, I had done so two years previously and despite the stress of the whole thing, successfully got through it, meaning I was eligible for promotion to uniform Sergeant anywhere in Bedfordshire.

A lot of my contemporaries would have given their eye teeth to be in that position, but absolutely not me. I loved what I was doing and even though deep down I knew it was a little short sighted, at that time I didn't see much point in deliberately not doing what I was enjoying for the sake of three stripes and the risk of doing an indeterminate number of years on shift work. My boss on the Drug Squad was extremely supportive and put forward a case for me to remain in the department as a DS, i.e., already in post so therefore familiar with current operations, fully trained and experienced, with a comprehensive knowledge of staffing issues. A summons to Police Headquarters at Kempston followed, where I saw the Chief Constable, Mr Alan Dyer, in his office. He indicated for me to sit down and there followed the strangest of conversations:

"So, Mr Dee, you're on the Drug Squad?"

"Yes, sir."

So far, so good. At least he knew where I was stationed. Turns out he knew considerably more than that.

"I see you passed your promotion exam some fifteen years ago?" I knew where this was going.

"Yes, I did, sir."

"Mmm... not risking getting killed in the rush to make Sergeant then?"

There was a slight smile on the Chief's face, and I wondered how to answer without dropping myself in it.

"Well sir," I ventured, "it does seem a shame there's no promotion structure within departments."

He was no longer smiling. Bugger. Had I gone too far?

"Can't have that." he frowned. "Creates a block and prevents others from having a shot at specialism." This wasn't going too well.

"And you," he went on, leaning forward across the desk and looking intently at me, "need to keep your horizons broadened."

This was it then, promoted into obscurity and shift work for heaven knows how long.

"Right, Mr Dee," he continued briskly, "I'm promoting you to the rank of Sergeant. Congratulations."

With that, the Chief stood up and extended his hand. I quickly rose from my chair and went to shake hands, but before I could do so, he barked, "Stay where you are!" Being halfway out the chair and not quite upright, I froze. What the hell's going on, I thought, why is he telling me not to move? The Chief was in exactly the same posture as me: leaning slightly forward across the desk with hand extended, neither of us moving. It was as if we were playing pass the parcel and the music had stopped. I was really confused and I thought afterwards that the Chief must have been wondering in that moment whether he'd promoted an imbecile. Of course, he'd simply meant 'Stay where you are on the Drug Squad…' It was a Private Pike moment. He went on to explain he had decided to make an exception about moving me from the unit on this one occasion as he was aware of how busy we were and the urgent need for a trained supervisor. The catch was that this would last for twelve months only, after which I would be moved to a uniform role elsewhere in the county. Oh well, I thought, at least it's a stay of execution. Again, a shame I couldn't have glanced into the future at that moment.

During my thirty-three years with Bedfordshire Police, I served under seven Chief Constables, and in my view, the most effective, and indeed caring, was Alan Dyer. I was to have a number of dealings with him and always found the man to be sincere, compassionate and with an amazing capacity for remembering details, particularly names. Each year on Christmas Day he would make it his business to personally visit each police station in the county, usually unannounced, and there were several amusing stories surrounding his arrival, particularly as he was rarely in uniform and new officers would fail to recognise him – not that there was ever an issue, his aim was simply to wish a Happy Christmas to those on duty and their families. One of life's gentlemen.

Soon afterwards, hardly having got used to promotion and the additional responsibility it entailed, I was whisked off to Dunstable for two months, seconded to a 'confidential' investigation along with Phil, an experienced and extremely effective divisional DC. We were under the direct supervision of the Detective Superintendent who was deputy head of the force CID, and the terms of reference related to investigating a series of night-time office burglaries committed throughout Leighton Buzzard town centre. The 'confidential' bit concerned the identity of the suspect: a serving Police Constable. This was one enquiry we weren't going to enjoy but of course the other side of the coin was that if there was a rotten apple in the barrel, it had to be exposed and dealt with.

Police officers' fingerprints are of course found at crime scenes for the simple reason that they are there on official business. If a fingerprint belonging to an officer is found at a crime scene and he had not been there on duty, it is fair to assume he had at some stage been present at that location whilst NOT on official police business. And so it proved. Such a mark was found by SOCO in an office at the scene of one of the burglaries.

One night, whilst this was still being investigated, a 'silent' burglar alarm was triggered at a solicitor's office in the town. 'Silent' meant no audible alarm at the premises, but an alert was transmitted to the police resulting in two officers speeding to the scene of the activation. They arrived within minutes and were in time to see the shadow of a person leaping from a window; the burglar heard their approach and was attempting to make his getaway. Although he landed badly and in fact sprained his ankle in the process, a combination of panic and adrenaline carried him away from the scene, managing to evade the pursuing officers.

A police driving course was taking place at the time and the following morning, one of the students telephoned in sick. With a sprained ankle. The fingerprint found at the scene of one of the burglaries was positively identified as belonging to that same officer and it was established beyond doubt he had not attended that particular burglary scene in the course of his duties nor in any other lawful capacity. The game was up. Following his arrest and charge, he was remanded in custody until his appearance at Snaresbrook

Crown Court in 1992 when he was convicted and sentenced to two and a half years' imprisonment.

His arrest had been a complete and utter shock to his colleagues on shift at Leighton Buzzard, especially when it became apparent that he had been committing at least some of the offences whilst on night duty alongside them. It took some time for his work mates to come to terms with the scale of his betrayal. "More than just a bent copper." one told me. "Far lower than that, he was a traitor working for the other side."

As recent events within the police service tend to demonstrate, much of the damage caused to the service by rogue officers is probably irreparable and makes the job of every honourable police officer that much more difficult.

Back with the Drug Squad, I was getting used to the anomalies of my new rank and actually beginning to see some of the logic behind being moved on promotion to a different arena of police work. Specialist units, particularly those involving mobile surveillance teams, work long unpredictable hours and camaraderie and friendship are essential elements. I was now in the position of supervising mates, checking their reports and writing staff appraisals, all of which to begin with, I found a tad awkward. But as things progressed, it became less arduous, mainly because the DCs knew their job well and were experienced in intelligence gathering and running their own operations including the management and handling of informants. Added to that, apart from some operational decisions, rank has no real part to play within an active surveillance team so I considered myself fortunate that my job on the Drug Squad remained largely the same as it had been prior to promotion.

The 'rave' scene nationally was now a huge problem for police and local authorities, the turning point being the May bank holiday of 1992 when in excess of 20,000 people converged on Castlemorton Common in the Malvern Hills. It began as a small free festival organised by the so-called New Age Travellers who hadn't banked on their event being hijacked by thousands of 'ravers' who'd heard about the festival via word of mouth, media coverage and a dedicated party telephone line. Facilities were utterly inadequate and the chaos that ensued from what was the largest illegal rave party in the UK ultimately resulted in a trial costing £4m and the passing of the Criminal Justice and Public Order Act 1994. The Act gave sweeping new powers to the police to prevent persons gathering for the purpose of a rave and to seize and retain vehicles and equipment intended for such a purpose.

The Home Office estimated that over a million Ecstasy tablets were being popped every weekend and cocaine use was vastly increasing with the UK on its way to being branded by the UN as 'Europe's cocaine capital'. It was an impossible tide and as a provincial drugs unit we could but chip away and try to destroy as much of the local illicit market as we were able to. The rave parties were at their height, with thousands of youngsters meeting at motorway service areas or industrial estates where, late at night, they would be given a venue location, usually by calling an answerphone. The raves were held in abandoned warehouses, fields or quarries and created a public order and safety nightmare for local authorities, landowners and police. As a Drug Squad, we were simply interested in the illegal use and distribution of drugs; it was not a case, as often alleged, of rave organisers being subjected to victimisation or harassment. If, as they maintained, raves had simply consisted of enabling youngsters to enjoy loud dance music in a spacious uninhibited disco-style environment, then they would have been of absolutely no interest to us.

One such organisation operated locally, attracting thousands of youngsters every fortnight to various locations around the region, routes and eventual addresses being revealed late in the evening to avoid detection by police. Most of the subsequent police intervention against them revolved around public order concerns as well as issues of trespass, but if specific intelligence was received relating to possible drug offences, then obviously we became involved.

As a result of information we received, a Misuse of Drugs Act search warrant was granted for a large residential premises taken over by the group and used as their home and headquarters. A number of the group were known to be present as they were preparing equipment for a rave party to be held elsewhere that evening, so a police operation was in place involving uniform officers and the Drug Squad. The warrant was executed and an extensive search of the premises conducted. A colleague, Dave, who was new to the squad, and I searched one of the bedrooms occupied at the time by one of the group organisers. We ensured that he was present throughout the search and drew his attention to what turned out to be a small quantity of cannabis and a number of MDMA (Ecstasy) tablets on a table next to the bed. When cautioned and asked to account for what we found, he became agitated, shouting that whatever the substance was, it was nothing to do with him, even though he had agreed that the room was solely occupied by him. He was arrested, taken to the police station and subsequently charged with possession of a Class A drug.

He pleaded not guilty at the subsequent Crown Court trial, the majority of the hearing revolving around issues of procedure at the police station and the detail of when and how the seized drugs were moved in and out of transit from a safe to the secure drug store and how those movements were recorded. The suggestion was made that the drugs were from elsewhere and so could not have been found at the house; in other words, Dave or I had 'planted' them. The confusion over the logging system evidence was sufficient to convince the jury that it was unsafe to bring in a guilty verdict and following a four-day trial, the defendant was found not guilty.

There is no doubt that the exhibit booking-in processes at the police station were at that time sufficiently lax as to allow defence counsel to exploit the inconsistencies and create enough doubt to make a conviction improbable.

Although the errors were purely administrative and neither fabricated nor dishonest, the group seized upon their 'success' at the trial to push for the instigation of a lawsuit against the police for wrongful arrest and falsification of evidence.

Many months later, I found myself standing in the witness box before a judge and jury in the Queens Bench Division of the High Court at The Strand in London. Cross-examination was conducted by a rather aggressive counsel who was trying to convince the court of the police's victimisation of the rave group in general and of the Drug Squad's 'evil intent' in particular. Again, the trial was all about the administrative cock up at the police station in relation to the continuity evidence of the drugs storage system, and of course if the court came to the conclusion that there was substance to the plaintiff's claim, i.e., no drugs were found at the house, then the consequences for Dave and me as individuals could be serious. This very eloquent barrister was doing his best to publicly discredit us as corrupt officers who had planted drugs on an innocent man.

Day two of my court interrogation resumed and my stress levels were compounded when I noticed the head of the Force Professional Standards department sitting in court. Professional Standards is the old Complaints and Discipline unit and is part of every force, employed to investigate complaints and allegations of misconduct against police. We knew of course the department would be keeping tabs on the trial, but to see the Superintendent actually in court awaiting the outcome was, to say the least, unnerving. If this went in favour of the plaintiff and the rave organisation was 'victorious', were we to be immediately suspended from duty? It didn't bear thinking about, surely that couldn't happen. Could it? We were innocent of any wrong-doing and our former defendant knew that just as well as we did. We could only wait for the justice system to take its course.

The rest of my cross-examination that day was a blur. I don't remember the detail of the questions but I do recall wondering whether the court was actually believing the barrage of ridiculous accusations that were coming my way; surely the jury could see through the smokescreen of hypothetical nonsense that was diverting attention from the truth? Having eventually finished my evidence, it was Dave's turn in the witness box to face the same questions under cross-examination about the supposed planting of drugs and alleged falsification of paperwork. At the time of the original search, although an experienced CID officer, Dave had joined the squad just one week earlier, and unsurprisingly hadn't expected the first drugs job he was involved in to be thrown out of court and then have to defend himself in the High Court against accusations of criminal activity!

The hearing dragged on for a week, but seemed like a month. On the Friday morning, with the verdict imminently expected, all interested parties were back at the Royal Courts of Justice, including, I noted, the Superintendent from Professional Standards. I hoped it wasn't an omen. An hour later, the sleepless nights and anxious days came to an end when the court dismissed the action and found in favour of the force. A huge relief that Dave and I, as individuals, had been properly vindicated and so by definition had the Drug Squad.

Through the late eighties and early nineties, the Drug Squad carried out many mobile surveillance operations and although constantly trying to identify the street dealers' own suppliers, the bread and butter of our work necessarily consisted of focusing on lower-level dealers and simply taking as many drugs off the street as we could. Of all those operations, one sticks in my mind for the odd way in which it concluded.

Informant-led intelligence came in that two addicts from 'somewhere around Milton Keynes' would be going to score a quantity of heroin from an unknown Luton address.

We needed to identify the premises and if circumstances were right, hit the address and carry out a search. We knew which day this was going to happen but that was all we had. The night before, the source got in touch and gave us an address in Bradwell, Milton Keynes from where the two potential targets would be leaving, although he couldn't yet help with identities or times. But we had a starting point for a mobile surveillance operation which was all we needed. Addicts are not known for early rising and as overtime was an issue, we took the decision to be on the plot at Milton Keynes for 8 am. Whilst during the RCS years we had only the force and car to car radios with which to communicate, technology had now progressed to the development of pocket pagers, so we could receive brief urgent text messages although if necessary, we still had to locate a payphone in order to respond to them. In this case, the source telephoned the office at 10 am to let us know the time of our targets' departure from Milton Keynes. A few minutes later, my pager buzzed with the message, 'Subjects leaving 1100hrs'. Excellent, good to have up-to-date information, especially when you have a whole team of detectives waiting to respond! We upped our concentration, fully aware that the commodity of time – and particularly punctuality – were alien concepts to addicts.

We needn't have worried; two scruffy individuals emerged from the address just after 11 am and went to a battered green Ford Escort parked down the road which we had identified as their potential transport. They were not looking around and showed no signs of being over-alert. We took them from the Bradwell area of Milton Keynes to the southbound M1 motorway where they pulled off onto the Toddington service area; the passenger got out and went to a public phone box, leaving the driver in the Escort with the engine running. This could be valuable intelligence for us, the normal procedure in these circumstances being that as soon as the targets left the area we would deploy an officer to the phone box to make a call to a random number, thereby 'marking' the call made by the target, i.e., when we acquired the schedule of calls, the number we wanted would be the one before our own and a GPO trace would give us the subscriber address.

After using the phone, our subject rejoined his mate in the Escort and they resumed their journey on the M1 towards Luton. We deployed an officer to the phone kiosk and the call was marked. Fortunately, the checks were not immediately necessary as our targets led us directly to the dealer's address in a Luton back street. The team covertly plotted up around the area, we had 'eyes' on the door to the address and waited for our two likely lads to emerge. Sure enough, ten minutes later, out they came, back to their Escort parked at the end of the street and away they went. But not far. We had arranged for a uniform patrol to do a hard stop on the vehicle and both were arrested in possession of a wrap of heroin apiece. Gathering our team together, we hit the address and it turned out the dealer was known to us: one Scott Willoughby. On piling through the door which led immediately into the lounge, there was Scott lying on a settee, obviously stoned, and a female sitting cross-legged on the threadbare carpet swaying to weird music and almost asleep; the smell of cannabis was overpowering. For what good it did, I explained the reason for our 'visit' to Scott and the lady and that they were both under arrest on suspicion of supplying a controlled substance. We had two female officers on the operation so both prisoners were able to be properly searched and handcuffed whilst we carried out an extensive search of the house.

We found a considerable amount of drugs paraphernalia such as hypodermic needles, syringes, silver foil and shoelaces (used as tourniquets) in various rooms as well as the final proof of dealing, half a dozen wraps of heroin in a box on the mantelpiece. Although you would expect to find these items in a drugs 'den', without doubt the most macabre find was a small glass phial inside some folded newspaper in a pocket of Willoughby's bomber jacket on the back of a chair. It was stuffed with blood-stained cotton wool. Fortunately, I was wearing latex gloves and made sure I didn't touch the phial itself.

"What the hell is this?" I asked.

"Get your hands off that," screamed Willoughby, "that's all I've got left of my friend!"

"What are you talking about?" I demanded, not wanting to know the answer.

"My mate Jason, died a month ago, he was HIV."

Unbelievably, it seems I'd found a sample of his dead mate's blood which was probably contaminated with the HIV virus and which this drug addled idiot was deliberately hanging on to. I could have understood a photograph in a locket or even stretched my understanding to a clip of hair, but this...

With the quantity of heroin found in the house and evidence from the two punters we had followed to the address, Willoughby was convicted of the supplying offence and sentenced to two years' imprisonment. The girl was found guilty of aiding and abetting and placed on probation for two years, the phial of bloodied cotton wool was incinerated, and I had a hepatitis B vaccination to be on the safe side.

Owing to the volume of drug cases for which we were producing sometimes complex court files, there would occasionally be a requirement for the officer in the case to attend a meeting with prosecuting counsel in his/her chambers, often at one of the four Inns of Court in London. I was fortunate enough to go to a number of such meetings over the years and I invariably found it an enjoyable and intriguing experience. The seven hundred-year-old history of a couple of the Inns in particular is fascinating and on one occasion I had the privilege of an unofficial guided tour of Lincoln's Inn in Holborn – I was amazed at the presence of eleven acres of delightful gardens in the centre of the City of London! The meetings often concluded with a little light refreshment at one of the nearby hostelries and it was one such occasion which led to an unfortunate episode during my return train journey to Bedfordshire.

The barrister and the solicitor I was with definitely enjoyed a tipple or two and as both were exceedingly good company and I was now off duty, it was no surprise that the afternoon and early evening flew by, leaving me eventually engaged in a disgustingly messy battle with a McDonald's cheeseburger before catching the Thameslink train from Kings Cross back to Luton. Coincidentally, on the platform I bumped into my squad colleague, Pete, hero of the Charlie Bronson incident, who was in London on another job, so we were able to keep each other company on the train back. As a result of the meeting that day, I must have been really tired. Pete told me later, "You passed out before the bloody train left Kings Cross."

Twenty minutes later, the train shuddered to a halt at Luton station and I woke up with a start, thanking my lucky stars Pete was there so I hadn't missed my stop. The doors opened and I gingerly stepped onto the platform, still a bit unsteady from my slumber. The doors slid closed behind me and it dawned on me that Pete wasn't there. I stood as if in a trance as the train pulled away, only to see Pete's grinning face peering through the window as he waved goodbye at me. What the hell's going on? I thought. Why didn't he get off the train with me? He's missed his stop. Then I saw the sign on the platform. Kentish Town. I wasn't at Luton at all, what a prat! Still, I reasoned, might be a bit of a wait but if I stay exactly where I am on this platform, I can get on the next train that comes along as all of them stop at Luton. It was a good plan and sure enough, fifteen minutes later, along came another train and I noticed it wasn't an express which would have gone non-stop to Bedford, so all was well. With a huge sense of relief, I slumped into a seat near the door and this time, I resolved to stay awake. Which I did for around five minutes. The next thing I was aware of was something nudging my foot which turned out to be a mop, and a cheerful Caribbean female voice said:

"Come on sir, you need to get off the train."

I dragged my eyes open, my head feeling as though it was having its own private disco. A cleaning lady was looking sympathetically down at me.

"So sorry," I mumbled. "Where are we?" I had the godfather of headaches.

"Brighton."

"WHAT?"

This wasn't possible, how had I got to the end of the Thameslink line at Brighton? I focused on my watch. Midnight. God, I was on duty in eight hours' time and I hadn't been home yet, Lynda would be worried sick. I needed to find a payphone quick, so thanking the lady for my early morning call, I vacated the carriage and found my way out of the station, thankfully without being challenged. A never to be forgotten phone call to Lynda followed and cutting a fairly traumatic tale short, I somehow got back to Luton railway station in the early hours of the morning, where the love of my life picked me up. I thought she couldn't have been too annoyed because on the drive home she didn't have a go at me, in fact she didn't say anything at all.

It didn't take a genius to work out what had happened at Kentish Town. As per my plan, I remained on the same platform to await my train's arrival, the problem being that in my state of confusion I turned 180 degrees, so although still on the same platform, I was facing the opposite direction and the train I staggered onto was travelling south and not north. An easy mistake to make. Especially for someone as tired as I was.

Chapter 14

Nine to Five

I remained with the Drug Squad for a total of six and a half years, which was quite unusual and undoubtedly to do with my unexpected promotion whilst on the unit. The one-year tariff stipulated by Mr Dyer had expired some eighteen months earlier and in the absence of any formal reminders from on high, I kept quiet. As I've said, the Drug Squad was one of the most enjoyable and rewarding parts of my service and I like to think we made something of a difference to the prevalence of drugs on the streets of Bedfordshire.

I was sorry to see the gradual demise of the squads nationally; drug offences were subsequently removed from national performance indicators and so were no longer considered a priority by individual forces. Statistically, it is effectively a victimless crime and therefore led to the unofficial but popular police observation, "You only have a drug problem if you look for it. The more we investigate drugs the more of a problem we find, and we have enough other priorities."

The inverted triangle of national drugs investigation organisations I mentioned earlier no longer exists – nowadays, the ultimate responsibility for drug trafficking investigations in the UK lies with the National Crime Agency, but at a national, more strategic level. Street drug crime is no longer looked into by a pro-active specialist unit; drug offences are dealt with by local resources reacting to a specific issue. The long-term effect of such a policy remains to be seen.

It was 1993 and rumours were rife that a strict tenure policy for specialist units was on the horizon, and it was generally accepted that it would be for three years. Bearing in mind the delicate situation concerning my own DS role, my thinking was that if tenure was enforced, I could well be on my way to shift work as a uniformed Patrol Sergeant for an indefinite period. Best to jump before pushed, and a job had been advertised for a provincial DS role within the National Drugs Intelligence Unit based at New Scotland Yard, a three-year secondment I would have loved, so I applied. It took less than a week for the application to be rejected by my own force, so it didn't even have the opportunity of being considered at a national level.

When I queried it, the reason became clear: I wasn't a 'substantive' Sergeant and hadn't attended any of the necessary training courses or management classes deemed to be necessary. Owing to the unusual method of my promotion, I'd slipped through the training net which I was pleased about in one way but now it had come back to bite me with the realisation that I wasn't eligible for outside postings!

My training 'shortfall' now highlighted, shortly afterwards I was sent to the Thames Valley Police Training Centre at Sulhamstead on a fortnight's 'Baby Sergeants' course. This was followed at Bedfordshire Headquarters by a management/leadership programme over three days, something I didn't particularly enjoy, but I did get introduced to some magnificently over the top managerial phrases, now common place but then were just becoming in vogue: 'Blue sky thinking', 'a window in your day', 'strategic staircase', and my personal favourite, 'thought shower', a successor to 'brainstorming'. Later on, I was an acting Inspector on a number of occasions and although my random use of such phrases in selected meetings ensured my own amusement, it did sometimes backfire.

I was acting DI on one occasion and attending a Headquarters management meeting about something or other. There were only four actual policemen at the meeting, including me, the remainder being from Specialist Crime Services admin and Human Resources. To say the meeting was boring is unfair, it was the stuff of slashed wrists and I couldn't wait for it to end. Being the afternoon, it began with an hour of struggling to keep my eyes from closing but then suddenly it was my turn to say something. I delivered some prepared facts about whatever the subject matter was, then for some reason I came out with, "It's about developing a push and pull strategy." Now, I've no idea what it meant or why I said it, I probably heard it on television the night before. The room went quiet then the Superintendent chairing the meeting said, "What strategy would that be then?" I needed a degree in waffle to get out of this one. I said something along the lines of, "Just a turn of phrase sir, I think we should seriously look at the existing strategy and see which bits of it need amending."

I had absolutely no clue what I was talking about and if there had been any further probing from the Chair or anyone else, I would have been in quite a dilemma. Fortunately, they all seemed to accept what I'd said, or more likely didn't want to hear any more rambling.

Now being a 'proper' Sergeant and supervisor, and nobody having mentioned Mr Dyer's edict about my promotion, I was qualified to apply for jobs in my rank and soon afterwards a vacancy was advertised in Force Orders for a DS office manager in the Force Intelligence Bureau (FIB) at Headquarters in Kempston. Although an office role, my CID status would be maintained, crime intelligence was a subject I knew something about and, I told myself, I'd had twenty-four years at the sharp end, so why not try for it?

It was a selection board interview process, which I absolutely hated, but having nothing to lose, I studied hard the things I thought I'd be asked about and applied for the job, as did three other candidates. The board went OK considering they didn't ask me a single question I thought they would; it was mainly about my career to date, which I easily talked through, plus a lot about my views on divisional liaison etc. Goodness knows how, but I got the job and so began three years of going home at the same time every evening and for the first twelve months it was brilliant, Lynda loved it and I found life much more relaxing with every weekend off and able to make plans I knew I could actually fulfil! No call outs, no cancelled rest days, no working 5 am till midnight. However, the downsides were little overtime, wearing a suit every day, no adrenaline rush and being a rather inconsequential cog in a world of management, corporate politics and administration.

What made it worthwhile were the people I worked with in the office, a mixture of police officers and support staff; the departmental boss was a DI with a brilliantly sarcastic turn of phrase and Martin, the office DC, was the mainstay and undoubted driving force of the everyday crime intelligence traffic that came through the Bureau. There were half a dozen support staff crime trend researchers, four of whom doubled as trained photo-fit, later e-fit, operators for the force. They would be summoned at all hours to attend stations around the county and spend as long as it took with a witness to compile an image of a suspect. They were professional and dedicated and two of them subsequently became serving police officers.

The set up with crime intelligence was that each divisional police station in the county had its own dedicated Local Intelligence Officer (LIO) with support staff where the size of the station allowed. The LIO was responsible for collating and disseminating intelligence from uniform patrols, CID and of course the general public. This would range from anything relating to crime suspects, the movement of local criminals, crime trends or anything else which might prove useful to a future operation or investigation. The role of the FIB was similar but with more of an overview of Bedfordshire crime and particularly where it transcended the borders with our neighbouring counties of Buckinghamshire, Northamptonshire and Hertfordshire. To that end, we held cross border meetings and conferences although I wasn't convinced they worked that well. I thought they needed to be more frequent and dynamic but as ever in the police service, politics and budgetary restraints often prevented us from doing what was probably best for the job.

Despite the lack of operational buzz, I learnt a lot during my time in the FIB and had experiences I would not otherwise have gained, some good, some not so good. The local BBC Three Counties Radio station had a regular spot where they discussed crime incidents and made appeals for witnesses etc. It was Martin's job to go along to the Bedford studio and do a ten-minute presentation about the latest goings on in the county, and he was very good at it. If he was off, it fell to me to broadcast to the nation (well, Beds, Herts and Bucks anyway). There's definitely a knack to doing a live radio interview and on my first effort in the studio, I left my knack in the office.

"So, here's Detective Sergeant John Dee from Bedfordshire Police Headquarters to tell us firstly about the series of distraction burglaries that have been occurring in Bedford." I froze. Of all my carefully prepared notes of the topics to be discussed, I knew there was nothing about distraction burglaries. All I knew from memory was there had been a spate of them in the Putnoe area of Bedford but that was the extent of my knowledge. In that moment, my mind flashed back to when I was twelve: it was Bingham village hall in Nottinghamshire, and I was taking part in a junior talent competition. My party piece was reciting monologues and I was doing Stanley Holloway's 'Albert and the Lion' in front of an audience of bored parents. The first line goes, 'There's a famous seaside place called Blackpool, that's noted for fresh air and fun,' and I delivered it confidently in a heavy northern accent which seemed to energise the audience slightly and I thought to myself how well it was going. And it probably would have done if I'd remembered the rest of the monologue.

My mind shut down and I couldn't remember a thing. Mum was at the side of the stage acting as my prompt, but after thirty seconds of frantically whispering the next line and me not hearing, her voice got louder until the audience could hear her calling out, "And Mr and Mrs Ramsbottom went there with young Albert, their son." That was one of my first trapdoor moments, and wasn't made easier when at the award ceremony afterwards, the local headmaster compering the evening suggested the fifth prize (there were only five of us in it) should go to my mum. Cheeky sod.

So here I was, thirty-five years on in a BBC studio, with that same sinking feeling; I'm supposed to speak live to hundreds of radio listeners concerning distraction burglaries, about which I know nothing. I had two options: come clean and admit I didn't have any details or make it up as I went along.

"Yes, there've been a number of them in the area." The words came out and I was committed. I had to follow up quickly with something that sounded as if I knew all about these burglaries before the interviewer could ask a more direct question.

"The thing about distraction burglary offenders," I went on, "is that they target the elderly, the vulnerable and people living alone. It's one of the most despicable of crimes and we're doing all we can in Bedford and elsewhere to catch the perpetrators."

The presenter seemed happy enough with that, but then he spoiled it by following up with, "Are there any descriptions of the suspects that we can help with circulating, Sergeant?" The one question I didn't want.

"We don't have a great deal of information on that score," I confidently spouted, "other than   two scruffy looking males, so please, particularly for those of your listeners in the Putnoe area, be on your guard and if you have any suspicions about unknown callers at your home, then don't hesitate to ring us."

I really had no idea about descriptions or even if there were any, so I decided to wing it and hope for the best. It seemed to work, the rest of the interview went OK and there were no repercussions from my office or the residents of Putnoe!

Operation Bumblebee was an anti-burglary campaign introduced initially by the Metropolitan Police in the early nineties to focus the public's attention on how to best protect their homes. The initiative also involved police

180

intelligence gathering operations aimed at the arrest of suspects. In addition, it co-ordinated regular 'roadshows' where thousands of pounds worth of recovered stolen property was displayed in an effort to have it identified and returned to its owners. The campaign was rolled out across London and subsequently taken up by several provincial forces, including Bedfordshire.

The popular TV police series, *The Bill* was running at the time and it was arranged for one of the stars, Andrew Paul, who played PC Dave Quinnan, to be invited to Police Headquarters to help launch our version of Operation Bumblebee. Andrew arrived in our office and it was clear he was very nervous about what was expected of him. He had joined the cast of *The Bill* some five years earlier, ostensibly for a three-month period, but remained with the programme for some thirteen years. He later said that his unique claim to minor fame was to be the only actor to have a part in *Inspector Morse* as well as the two spin offs, *Lewis* and *Endeavour*. One of my favourite TV cop shows of all time is *The Sweeney* and I was impressed to learn that Andrew had also had a part in the very final episode, shown in December 1978.

He needn't have been so apprehensive about our little operation, the launch at Headquarters with the local press and TV went really well and our campaign hugely benefitted from his celebrity status.

One of my roles at the FIB was that of Interpol Liaison Officer for the force, effectively being the point of contact if an international crime enquiry needed to be facilitated within the county or if we had a local investigation necessitating further enquiries abroad. The International Criminal Police Organisation has its headquarters in Lyon and exists to facilitate worldwide police co-operation, investigative support and training. One of the commitments of my role was to attend the annual Interpol Liaison Officers' conference in London and one of these fell shortly after the Bumblebee launch. Representatives from many forces attended the event which involved presentations by various Interpol staff and included a lunch and usually a guest speaker. On this occasion, the speaker was author Colin Dexter, the creator of *Morse*, which at the time was at the peak of its TV success. Like his starring character, Colin was a keen real ale drinker and fuelled by a few pints gave an excellent speech, full of amusing anecdotes and on-set trivia. We met briefly afterwards and exchanged pleasantries; who'd have thought that a quarter of a century later, in my second life as a TV extra, I'd have a walk on part in *Endeavour,* the popular *Morse* spin-off series.

On one of numerous visits to New Scotland Yard, then situated at Broadway in the City of Westminster, I was lucky enough to visit the Metropolitan Police Black Museum in room 101, an intriguing exhibition of crime exhibits first opened in1874 as the Central Prisoners' Property Store where police collected items of prisoners' property for instructional purposes. Not being open to the public and with entry by invitation only, I was fortunate to have a friend stationed at NSY who arranged for a small group of us to attend. It was a fascinating experience with displayed items ranging from various murder weapons to artefacts from infamous cases such as Jack the Ripper, John Christie and Dr Crippen. It even featured the stove and saucepans used by serial killer Denis Nilsen to cook the body parts of some of his dozen or so victims. As well as the intrigue of such macabre items as the death masks of those hanged at Newgate Prison and the collection of original hangmen's nooses, I'll never forget the contents of one particular display cabinet. The uniform worn by PC Keith Blakelock on the night he lost his life in the Broadwater Farm riots at Tottenham on 6th October 1985. His tunic was covered with pieces of white laboratory tape indicating more than forty holes where he had been repeatedly stabbed.

The details of the horror of that night are well known but I make no apology for repeating them; we must never forget what happened to one of our own in twentieth century London at the hands of a killer mob.

In the midst of the rioting, a group of firefighters were attempting to put out a blaze in a shop on the estate when they came under attack from rioters; a group of police officers, including PC Blakelock, were detailed to protect them. The situation escalated and the police and firefighters began to withdraw, with Keith and a colleague, PC Richard Coombes, becoming separated from the other officers. Witness reports state that a group of forty to fifty people closed in on the pair and attacked them with sticks, bottles, knives and machetes. Keith died of horrific injuries and was found with a knife still embedded up to the hilt 6 inches into his neck. At one of the subsequent court hearings, it was stated that it was believed an attempt had been made to decapitate him. Miraculously, PC Richard Coombes survived but received such severe injuries that he never returned to active duty. Despite a series of trials, including the conviction of three men in 1987 which was subsequently overturned on appeal, no one to date has been found guilty of Keith's murder.

Looking at the remains of the tunic was a shock and the silence in the room became almost tangible as we gazed at this manifestation of the evil that had befallen one of our comrades. There but for the grace of God.

One of the subsidiary FIB responsibilities was to carry out training classes for new recruits on the subject of criminal intelligence: what it is, how it is acquired, processed and disseminated for action. Martin and I would take it in turns to run the sessions for one- or two-hour periods and I have to say, I enjoyed them. The students were young probationer constables with less than two years' service, and our sessions were a part of their ongoing training. I think they tended to enjoy our input; they knew it would be of everyday practical value to them and we did our best to make the sessions relative to real life situations they would potentially come across. I would always conclude with a lengthy question and answer period, my view being that this was such an important area of policing that the students really needed a thorough understanding of the subject, and their questions would not only demonstrate whether or not they had a grip of it, but also gave me an opportunity to give some practical answers and scenarios based on my own experience. There was never a shortage of questions and my allotted session time often overran. The training periods went well and the feedback we received from the students via the training department was always very positive.

One afternoon, I went across as usual to the Headquarters' training department for a 2 pm to 3.30 pm session with a class of a dozen or so probationers; as I walked into the classroom I was aware one of the trainers was sitting at the back of the room. Not a problem, the class instructors were sometimes present to introduce whoever was doing the presentation and would then leave us to our own devices. This particular instructor, perched comfortably on the edge of a table, was obviously going nowhere.

"Ok John?" she said. "Just sitting in."

"No worries," I replied, "but no heckling please."

I grinned at her but it wasn't reciprocated. Although her presence didn't bother me, I did wonder why she had nothing else to do. Still, on with the show.

The session followed the normal format, beginning with my usual opener, "Can anyone tell me the difference between information and intelligence?" This always got them thinking and the answer is crucial to the understanding of what crime intelligence is all about. I noticed the instructor busily scribbling away on a clipboard, presumably noting down which of the students were reacting or otherwise. Several responses were forthcoming, some good ones, some a long way off the mark. As I'd hoped, it sparked an animated discussion in which all of the students took part and eventually, with a little prompting, they arrived at the right answer. More importantly from my point of view, they now had a better understanding of what crime intelligence was all about before we moved on to the rest of the session.

I showed a short film on how military commanders gathered and utilised intelligence, followed by an input on how, as police officers, we need the raw intelligence material transformed into evidence. The lesson concluded with my usual twenty minutes of questions and answers, followed by a "Thanks for your time," from the instructor. And that was that. Or so I thought.

Several days later I got a phone call in the office asking if I could pop down to the training department to see the instructor who had sat in on my probationer input. It was a particularly busy day in the FIB, we were co-ordinating a number of live operations at the time and the phones were jumping, but during a lull, I decided to go down and quickly find out what they wanted. The instructor was on her own in the office and beckoned me to sit down.

"John, how are you?"

"OK, thanks. Problem?" I wanted to get back to the office.

"Not a problem, no, just a quick chat really about how you thought the last input went?"

"I thought it went OK, didn't you?"

"Generally, yes, just some points to make you aware of." She smiled, only this time it was my turn not to reciprocate. What was she talking about?

"We have to try and standardise the training we give," she went on, "and I appreciate you've had no formal instruction, just that you were maybe a little too familiar with the students on Tuesday."

I felt the hackles begin to rise. So that was it, she had been assessing me, not the probationers.

"Too familiar? What the hell does that mean?"

"Well, only that we should maintain an instructor/student relationship in the classroom, and I did feel you perhaps overdid the laughing and joking aspect when you were describing some of the operations you've been involved in."

Hackles now fully risen.

"Look," I said, struggling to control my annoyance. "I know I'm not a trained teacher but I do know about criminal intelligence and the operations I spoke about were only successful because of it. What's wrong with getting that across?"

"Nothing at all," came the reply. "Just the method of delivery needs a little adjusting and maybe not so much of the colourful language."

Colourful language? As far as I could recall, the occasional 'bloody' was as far as it went.

Obviously even that was too bloody far. I wondered if probationer constables were still subject to the rigorous military style introduction at training centres that my generation was, not to mention the 'colourful language' used by the Drill sergeant.

So, there it was, swearing in the classroom and too friendly with the natives. Rightly or wrongly, I'd had enough.

"OK, maybe you have a point, but just a couple of things. As you said, I've had no formal instruction in teaching methods but you knew that when we were asked to do these presentations and I've been doing them for the last eighteen months without any criticism; in fact, from the student feedback sheets I've seen, they've gone down well. So, what prompted the training department to suddenly question my ability to do them?"

The trainer appeared momentarily taken aback, then she replied:

"John, your ability and experience were never in question, it's simply a matter of instruction being delivered in an appropriate manner, and following a comment from a previous student it was decided that outside speakers would be monitored to make sure the classes are receiving just that." Now it was clear.

"So, one of them took exception to something I said?"

She didn't answer that one, but it didn't really matter, my mind was made up. Probably cutting off my nose to spite my face, but that was the last probationer constable input I did. I knew I couldn't do them justice if my every move and comment were going to be 'monitored' and subject to scrutiny. A shame, I'd enjoyed doing them and more importantly, I know the students had too.

But the training department did prove useful in other ways. One of the advantages of doing straight eight-hour days in the FIB office was that I was able to get myself on an Assessors course which was two weeks of training at headquarters, at the conclusion of which, if successful, one is qualified to sit on the other side of the desk at internal selection boards. The course was actually quite enjoyable and I gained a lot from it, not the least of which was first-hand knowledge of the process, from the application sift and shortlist mechanism to the various marking systems against which the final decision was made. Assessors were trained from every background, including specialist units such as the Dog Section and Road Traffic and included civilian police staff, so the majority of interview panels provided a good mix of knowledge and experience. I was used many times as an assessor on internal interview boards and it supplied me with a valuable insight into the dos and don'ts of applying for a specialist post. It was to be a useful arrow in my quiver.

Chapter 15

The Emerald Isle

After three years of nine-to-fives wandering the corridors of power at Headquarters, I began to look around for operational DS jobs, both in-force and externally. Sadly for the force, the Chief Constable, Alan Dyer, had recently retired and still no mention had been made by anyone of a sideways move into uniform for me, so as it was now more than five years since my promotion, it was fair to assume that my chat with the Chief in his office that day about staying as a DS for only twelve months had not been formally recorded. Intentional or not, I was extremely grateful!

One day I received a phone call from one of the detectives on Special Branch (SB), telling me that a vacancy for a DS would shortly be available and the role would involve the supervising of operations and running their surveillance team, if I was interested in applying. If I was interested? I had always liked the idea of Special Branch, my only reservation was that owing to the existence of Luton airport, the force was funded to provide a SB presence twenty-four hours a day, on shift work. That I didn't fancy, it was too much akin to my early experience in the Air Force Department Constabulary of being in one place and involved in fairly repetitive practices: in this case, the checking of manifests and manning entry control points at flight arrival areas etc. Nothing wrong with the role of course, it was a really important job at the time, just not my cup of tea. But the department had two DSs, one being responsible for the SB contingency at the airport and the other, the job on offer, was based at Luton Police Station overseeing a team engaged on the operational side of Special Branch work. It was a comparatively rare opportunity and I felt it was right up my street. The only issue, again, was getting through the selection board process, but at least this time, hopefully, I had something of an advantage being an assessor myself. Or so I told myself.

I got through the paper sift OK, which left half a dozen of us to prepare for the interview; the problem facing us was exactly which areas to research, as Special Branch by its nature was basically a 'closed shop'. It was 1996 and being pre-Google, Wikipedia and most things digital, we needed to acquire as much physical reading material as we could, as well as separately canvassing those SB members we knew individually in an effort to learn what the department was all about. Irish terrorism was top of their work agenda and with a strong Irish community in Luton, the SB intelligence gathering capability was paramount, as was a close relationship with the Security Service (MI5) and the Metropolitan Police Special Branch (MPSB).

It was a particularly sensitive time as in February that year, the Provisional Irish Republican Army (PIRA) ended their eighteen-month long ceasefire by detonating a truck bomb in the London Docklands at South Quay, near Canary Wharf, killing two people and injuring over a hundred as well as causing £150m worth of damage. Security levels were at maximum and all Special Branches were on high alert, particularly those forces with responsibility for port policing; and Luton, of course, was under the spotlight because of the airport's direct flight link to Ireland.

The day of the interview arrived, and I went along with a head full of facts and figures on the history of the Troubles in Northern Ireland including details of the various republican and loyalist paramilitary groups. I had also studied the growing threat from Islamic terrorism as well as gathering a basic understanding of how Special Branches fit into the national scheme of things. I thought I was pretty well prepared, but ten minutes in, I felt the same apprehension I'd experienced on my last interview for the FIB job three years earlier. I don't remember exactly what the questions were from the panel, but I do know they had nothing to do with all the stuff I had spent weeks studying;

there was a lot on management style and hypothetical supervisory problems with staff and at the end of the interview I just hoped I'd done enough and that perhaps my practical experience might carry me through.

When I got the phone call a week later from the Head of Special Branch (HSB) Detective Inspector to tell me I'd got the job, I began to think maybe I was better at selection boards than I thought! I had to admit it was a relief that I wouldn't be spending the next part of my service in an office somewhere or as a uniform shift Sergeant, but the real bonus for me was that I'd be doing a job that had always intrigued and to which I felt suited.

Special Branch has traditionally been regarded as something of an enigma within the police service, which is not surprising owing to the level of personal vetting required and the covert nature of much of its work. I was also amazed to learn of a perception amongst certain sections of the public that SB was nothing to do with the police and was an independent government security organisation! The truth of course is that, certainly in the provinces, SB is simply a department within the CID in the same way as the Drug Squad or the Fraud Squad under the command of the force Detective Chief Superintendent. Its 'secret squirrel' persona is inevitable given the sensitivity of the material to which its officers have access and the covert nature of how they need to respond to what is known as the security requirement.

The organisation was formed by the Metropolitan Police in 1883 and called the Special Irish Branch, having been brought into being to combat the Irish Republican Brotherhood. Later, as its area of responsibility was extended to include more than Irish Republican related counter espionage, it became known simply as Special Branch. In subsequent years, each force throughout the UK formed its own SB in response to the growing threat from subversive elements around the world, its role being to assess and develop intelligence of a political or sensitive nature. It also investigated potential threats to the State from terrorism or extremist political activity, all carried out under the auspices of the Security Service (MI5).

Sympathisers with various political ideological causes exist everywhere but only create a problem if they progress their allegiances to illegal or subversive activity, which is where the Special Branches come into play: the results of their local knowledge and intelligence gathering capabilities contribute significantly to the overall national picture. Additionally, those suspected of being involved directly or in support of terrorism and reside in a particular force area will automatically be of significant interest to that force's Special Branch.

Any officer joining a specialist unit must have adequate training for the role, none more so than Special Branch. Following an extensive government vetting interview, each new member was required to attend a two-week initial SB course at New Scotland Yard (NSY) co-hosted by a senior MPSB officer and a member of the Security Service training department. The course included a number of inputs on the management of informants, or as MI5 preferred to call it, agent handling. We were particularly fortunate in having two members of the Royal Ulster Constabulary (RUC), renamed in 2001 as the Police Service of Northern Ireland (PSNI), on our course, both being experienced agent handlers and very much at the 'sharp end' in Belfast. Most on the course had varying degrees of experience in running informants but none of us would claim to compare with the two RUC men, both already tried and tested Special Branch officers. One of them in particular was a DCI for whom everyone, including the course instructors, had a huge amount of respect. His experience of agent handling was phenomenal and he was able to inject almost every class session with real life practicalities, invaluable for the rest of us. It was widely accepted that RUC officers had no specific need for such training, they attended these courses to gain a short respite from the full-on workload and everyday stress of dealing with sources within the paramilitary organisations on both sides of the political divide.

I enjoyed the course, which included an introductory visit to MI5 headquarters at Thames House, near Lambeth Bridge, a twenty-minute walk from NSY and the first of many visits to the Security Service HQ. Intriguingly, Thames House affords a view across the river of the headquarters of its sister organisation, the Secret Intelligence Service (SIS) or MI6, located at Albert Embankment next to Vauxhall Bridge and the backdrop for a number of James Bond films such as *Goldeneye*, *Die Another Day* and *Skyfall*.

Both organisations, along with the Government Communications Headquarters (GCHQ) at Cheltenham, form the basis of the United Kingdom's intelligence machinery network. MI5 is the domestic counter-intelligence and security agency, whilst MI6 operates overseas in its role as the UK's foreign intelligence service. During my time with Special Branch, although we had a number of dealings with MI6 when our work impacted on ongoing operations abroad, the vast majority of time was spent working alongside MI5 case officers and their surveillance teams.

Broadly, Bedfordshire SB was divided into two areas of responsibility, with half the unit based at Luton airport and the rest as an operational team of eight or so detectives working from Luton Police Station supervised by a DS (my role) with the essential administrative responsibility carried out by an experienced DC and two civilian staff.

Whilst the force held in-house courses in mobile surveillance, our Special Branch was privileged to have such training supplemented by A4, the Security Service department responsible for their own surveillance capability. These were unique opportunities and, outside London, so far as I was aware, only existed for Bedfordshire, testament to the strong working relationship between our two organisations. The training supplied by A4 was particularly valuable to our unit owing to their vast experience in carrying out operations directed at terrorist organisations as well as against individuals deployed by foreign powers considered a threat to UK security.

Of course, being a government service, they had access to a great deal of equipment and resources including vehicles, helicopters and, naturally, all manner of covert listening devices, which, by default, often became available for our use.

Back from my course, the first job I became involved in was an already ongoing case concerning an individual believed to be an active member of the PIRA organisation in Northern Ireland. Intelligence had been received from the RUC that he was making regular trips from Belfast to the mainland, usually via Luton airport, and was believed to be involved in PIRA business whilst doing so. Our brief from MI5 was to gather as much intelligence on his activities as we could, which necessitated keeping him under surveillance each time he landed at Luton. There were many long days and evenings in which our target spent a lot of time in Luton's Irish pubs and clubs and we collected a great deal of information about his associates, contacts and habits. One of the principles of surveillance is to always remain conscious that a target can rapidly jump on a train or into a taxi, and within minutes be miles away from an unwary surveillance team.

One day, without warning, our target collected a hire car and drove over two hundred miles to the coast to meet a contact. Together with assistance from two other Special Branches, we kept control of him for the entire journey, monitored his stops and successfully identified the addresses he visited. However, it was a difficult surveillance: the distance involved increased the risk of target loss, particularly at night, and also being a suspected member of a paramilitary organisation, he was more than likely to have received some form of anti-surveillance training, so we needed to be extra vigilant throughout the four or five hours of the operation to ensure none of our team was open to compromise.

We were 'with' the man for several months on and off and we learned from other sources that he usually felt safe when on the mainland and at no time during any of the operations against him did we receive feedback to suggest he had been aware of our presence. During this operation, along with one of our team, I had the privilege of going to Northern Ireland for a few days to work alongside the RUC Special Branch and to observe at first hand the conditions under which they operated and the very real dangers they encountered on a daily basis. They were constantly armed, including when driving to and from home, and it was a jolt to realise that we were all in the same United Kingdom law enforcement business and working for the same results, but in completely different environments.

Hard to imagine having to routinely carry out anti-surveillance measures in my own vehicle on leaving work for the day, and the next morning checking the underside of my car in case someone had planted an improvised explosive device (IED). It was the mid-1990s and this was life in the RUC on British soil, just three hundred and twenty miles from London.

Once our briefing, intelligence exchange and planning was complete for the day, and being our first visit to Ireland, we were taken on a tour of West Belfast to see the murals and peace walls of the Falls and Shankill Roads. The Good Friday Agreement was in the future and each time we stopped to cautiously pose for a quick photograph beside one of the huge murals, our armed hosts were noticeably wary, constantly ushering us back to the car. In the Falls Road I stayed a little too long looking at the huge painting of Bobby Sands when an Irish voice immediately behind me hissed, "Get in the car JD, it's fairly safe here, but not that f….. safe!" A fascinating guided tour that afternoon, albeit an uneasy one.

The evening was a far more relaxed affair, in fact, by midnight we were extremely relaxed... Some say the Guinness in Ireland is no different to that on the mainland; I'm no expert and I have no idea if that is true or not, all I can report is that the effect of a gallon plus of the stuff in Ireland has exactly the same effect as it does in England. The RUC were expert 'socialisers', really looking after us in terms of food and drink and the only items missing from the experience were chunks of memory the following day. Which was unfortunate, because early the next morning, the second part of our visit to the province was an intelligence gathering trip around the haunts of our target. In a helicopter.

Years later, following my retirement, Lynda and I went on an amazing tour of Canada and Alaska, and one of the experiences that will remain with me always was a flight in a glass bottomed helicopter over the Rocky Mountains. I can recall every second of the experience, backed up by our countless photographs. But I certainly don't need photographs to remember details of the Ireland trip our army helicopter crew took us on that morning. Other than the pilot, aboard the helicopter were the two of us, a pair of RUC SB guys and two soldiers who continually manned a general purpose machine gun (GPMG) pointed at the ground through the helicopter's open hatch for the duration of the flight. I was seated by the hatch with a bird's eye view and the soldiers' attention never strayed from watching every inch of the ground as we sped swiftly over the fields and urban areas of Ulster. Their vigilance was reassuring, at least five military helicopters had been shot down by Irish Republican paramilitaries over the preceding years, with many more incidents of being under sustained fire from mortar attacks, heavy machine guns and even surface-to-air-missiles. In this region, there was no such thing as guaranteed safe air space.

It was a fascinating exercise and once we had noted and photographed what was needed, we began the return trip to base. The pilot was obviously aware of our previous evening's 'social networking' event with his RUC mates and decided to have some fun with our digestive systems. We 'hurdled' nearly all the way back, which, as the name suggests, meant we flew at low altitude over fields and open ground until we came to trees and hedgerows, at which point we rapidly climbed and then dropped again. This hedgehopping was clearly designed as a breakfast re-introduction strategy, and we were pleased and relieved to say that it failed. But only just! Our trip had been an absorbing introduction to this land and was the first of my many visits to the gorgeous island of Ireland.

Luton was a focal meeting point for various members of Irish Republican paramilitary groups, and although we were usually made aware when these individuals were due to arrive in the town, our problem was establishing whether they were there 'on business' or for social reasons. Mobile surveillance was often the only option at our disposal.

Early one Friday morning, we received intelligence from the Security Service that 'X', a senior PIRA player, was due to arrive at Luton airport at a particular time and would be taking part in some sort of meeting with others unknown in one of the town's pubs. This was coupled with unverified information that at the same time, a vehicle kitted with explosives would be arriving from Ireland into the UK via 'somewhere along the west coast', possibly Holyhead, but not confirmed, and then driven to an unknown location north of London for a period of storage before being deployed. It was alleged to be a lorry bomb, known as a vehicle borne improvised explosive device (VBIED) and the information was treated as high priority, not least because the world was still in a state of shock from the atrocity of the Omagh bombing earlier in the year: twenty-nine innocent people lost their lives and over two hundred were injured in the car bomb blast for which PIRA splinter group, the Real Irish Republican Army (RIRA), claimed responsibility. It was the single most deadly bombing of the Troubles; six children and a woman pregnant with twins were amongst those who died. The death toll included eighteen Catholics and eleven Protestants and did nothing to enhance the RIRA's cause.

Although no specific information existed linking our man to the VBIED, it was a coincidence that could not be ignored. The Security Service deployed a team to Holyhead and with A4's assistance, we deployed our team at Luton airport to await the arrival of X, who duly arrived on a scheduled easyJet flight early on the Friday evening. For the majority of the weekend, we stayed with X whilst he drank and gambled his way around Luton's Irish pubs and betting shops. By the time Sunday evening arrived, he'd consumed his own weight in Guinness and Jameson whiskey, and although we had gathered a great deal of information about his drinking partners and their vehicles etc., we were operationally no further forward. The VBIED did not arrive and our overtime budget was shattered for the remainder of that financial year! Some you win.

Chapter 16

Defence of the Realm

A major asset for any detective officer is the ability to identify, cultivate and recruit informants from within the criminal fraternity. Naturally, some officers are more successful at this type of work than others, and it can be a minefield if the stringent regulations governing the use of informants are not strictly adhered to. In fact, it's a minefield even when they ARE adhered to. The current guiding statute is the Regulation of Investigatory Powers Act 2000 (RIPA) to which all law enforcement agencies and the Security Services are subject. Special Branch officers require specific training in relation to informant handling, and although the principles are the same, the courses run by MI5 for SB officers necessarily incorporate anti and counter-surveillance training as well as practice in what are called brush contacts (BC) and dead letter boxes (DLBs). A BC is simply where a brief and often public meeting takes place in which two individuals discreetly exchange items, usually money or instructions, without acknowledging each other. A DLB is a place where messages can be left and collected without the sender and recipient meeting. The anti and counter-surveillance measures are necessary for the agent handler and the agent to be sure they are not followed to the meeting.

The SB agent handling courses were of two weeks' duration, the first half being conducted from MI5 HQ at Thames House and the second week consisting of intense practical exercises in and around a selected city. The practicals were played for real with a team of A4 officers carrying out surveillance on the students, although they were never told when. The 'agents' were MI5 role players and our task was to cultivate them, assess their potential usefulness to the UK, then hopefully recruit and direct them.

The BCs and DLBs were still useful concepts in the nineties when mobile phones were a luxury, the internet was in its infancy and social media platforms non-existent; so, the tried and tested means of clandestine communication were still being used to good effect. But they required practice and skill to get right, as indeed did the anti and counter-surveillance techniques, which we frequently used on live operations to ensure the safety of both established and prospective agents. All of these skills come under the banner of 'tradecraft' and there are no better exponents than A4.

Whilst in a Midlands city during the exercise part of my own course, one of the tasks was to plan and execute a brush contact with my agent; it was to be the handover of a film cannister from me to him in a public location selected by me. We had practised BCs earlier in the course and I was reasonably confident of carrying out the task quickly and without being observed. There were half a dozen students operating in various areas of the city, and obviously not all of us were under surveillance at the same time, but we could never be certain if A4 were watching or not.

My agent was role playing as a close friend of a member of Hizb ut-Tahrir, a political organisation committed to the establishment of shariah law within the Muslim community and I needed to get some urgent written instructions to him. I made a recce of the city centre and selected a public stairwell belonging to a multi-storey car park for the transfer. I contacted the agent and gave him precise instructions: he was to go up the stairway from the street at exactly 2 pm and would pass me coming down from the top level of the car park and I would slip the cannister to him, there appearing to be no contact between us. He was to continue up to the car park where his vehicle was parked.

At 1.55 pm, I drove my car onto the top level of the car park and parked up adjacent to the stairwell. I had driven an anti-surveillance route, did not detect being followed and no other vehicles had come with me into the parking area. Checking my watch, I began the stairwell descent, walking quite quickly as per the plan. Three flights down, I saw my agent coming up towards me. We avoided eye contact and as we drew level, without slowing, I pushed the cannister from my right hand into his right hand. It took less than a second, and we continued our respective ways. The agent's timing had been spot on, he'd followed instructions to the letter and I was pleased with the location I'd chosen – although public, it was secure enough for the BC to have taken place without being observed.

The evening came, time for our daily debrief, where our success, or otherwise, was discussed. The students sat in a semicircle with the course instructors at the front. I was first on. When it came to my brush contact, Alan, the chief instructor, asked how it had gone. I said I thought it went reasonably well and that anti-surveillance prior to the meeting had satisfied me there was no one following.

"OK," he replied, "and how did the actual brush go?"

"Fine. The timing was good, it was quick and we weren't observed."

He smiled. "OK, come in," he called loudly. My stomach tightened; I had a feeling this wasn't going to go too well. The classroom door opened and in walked a small, elderly lady.

"JD, meet Ruth from A4," Alan said.

"Hello again." Ruth smiled. Then it hit me. Charging down the car park stairs, I vaguely remembered on the second level stepping quickly past an old lady struggling with a shopping bag and thinking that under normal circumstances I'd have helped her, but timing was everything on the exercise and I couldn't afford to stop.

"I'd never have sussed you as surveillance in a hundred years," I said, shaking my head, "but you couldn't have clocked the handover, you were way behind me on the stairs?"

Ruth smiled again. "You mean the little black package you handed to the Asian guy halfway down?"

"Bugger," I muttered. "How did you see that?"

"Stayed one flight of stairs behind, just out of your view, and each flight curves around slightly so I could see through to the set of stairs below me."

Sounded simple, but it demonstrated how good A4 are. The learning point was that every contact with an agent/informant, whether an arranged briefing meeting or a quick casual street meeting, must be made with the safety and security of the agent as a priority. Ensuring beyond doubt that there is no surveillance is paramount.

MI5 is fortunate in that it is able to draw upon males and females of all ages, sizes and backgrounds as part of its surveillance capability, whilst a police unit, particularly in those days, was restricted to whatever age, height and fitness requirements their particular forces were subject to. The advantages of training individuals of any physical dimensions, even those with a visible disability, to be able to instantly blend into almost any background are obvious, and Ruth was a case in point!

But it was not always so. Prior to 1975, the Security Service was no different to other organisations of the time and sex discrimination was rife. Although women were recruited onto the surveillance units, they were not allowed to remain permanently, and incredibly, one of the Service Directors wrote in 1967:

'*Once we allow a woman to stay for over five years we should find it very difficult in practice to get rid of her at all.*'

The author would probably have killed himself with a poison-tipped umbrella had he known that twenty-five years later MI5 would appoint its first female Director General.

Through the 1990s, MI5 knew that the main terror threat to Britain, apart from Irish Republican dissidents, was from assorted Islamic extremist groups, some of which were prominent in London, Birmingham, Manchester and significantly for us, Luton. One such organisation was Al-Muhajiroun, a group dedicated to the creation of an Islamic state in Britain with the abolition of democracy and the introduction of shariah law. A great deal of our time was spent monitoring individuals known to belong to the movement and investigating their activities and associates. A number of operations inevitably came to nothing but some members of the groups we were interested in would become major players on the stage of international terrorism in later years. One such individual was Mustafa Kamel Mustafa, better known as Abu Hamza al Masri, who, from 1998, was the imam of Finsbury Park Mosque in London. In the mid-nineties, the one-eyed, hook-handed cleric was a frequent visitor to Bedfordshire, and Luton in particular, and his associates and movements were increasingly the subject of our attention. He was known to preach his radical fundamentalist views at various mosques and of course, once he became imam at Finsbury Park, was able to spread his message of hate to a wider audience. A great deal of intelligence work and evidence gathering over a number of years by Special Branches and the Security Service finally resulted in Hamza facing trial at the Old Bailey in February 2006. He was found guilty on six charges of soliciting murder, three charges of using threatening words or behaviour with intent to stir up racial hatred, one charge of possessing threatening, abusive or insulting sound recordings with intent to stir up racial hatred and one charge of possessing a document containing information likely to be useful to a person committing or preparing an act of terrorism. He was sentenced to seven years' imprisonment, following which, in October 2012, he was extradited to the USA where he was subsequently convicted of eleven further charges relating to hostage taking, conspiring to establish a military training camp and calling for war in Afghanistan. He was sentenced to life imprisonment without parole.

Bedfordshire Special Branch was involved in many similar intelligence gathering operations and offshoot investigations, all of which, to a greater or lesser extent, fed into the national intelligence picture. Our unit ran a number of sources with varying degrees of access and reliability, from those with an Irish background through to public spirited Asian citizens who did not approve of the views expressed by potentially dissident individuals in their midst. Sources were also cultivated from those within or on the fringes of local animal rights extremist groups; part of the SB remit was to monitor such activity and to gather intelligence which would assist in the prevention of attacks on persons or property targeted by these individuals. The Metropolitan Police co-ordinated this intelligence from the Special Branches of all forces so a national picture of possible extremist activity could be formulated.

I had been in Special Branch barely eighteen months when an unprecedented problem arose relating to a major target operation we were running at the time. The target was a suspected foreign intelligence officer living in temporary accommodation in the county and was the subject of a long-term joint investigation by ourselves and MI5. The operation had been running for some twelve months and was proving successful in terms of useful intelligence. In August 1997, one of the MI5 desk officers previously involved with the case turned 'whistle-blower' and made allegations to the national press citing a series of supposed misdeeds by the security services, ranging from an allegation of a failed assassination attempt by MI6 on a foreign leader, to MI5 carrying out surveillance operations against high profile politicians as well as on show business personalities. The accusations involved a degree of detail about the 'mishandling' of some ongoing investigations, including our own. This could have resulted not only in the abandoning of our operation but in serious consequences for some of the individuals involved. However, as luck would have it, no great harm was done and the whistle-blower was later arrested, convicted for three offences of breaking the Official Secrets Act and imprisoned. But it was an anxious time, there are enough dangers relating to classified operations conducted under normal circumstances without having to worry about betrayal from within the heart of our own intelligence services!

One day I received a phone call from one of the A4 team leaders to ask if I could supply a surveillance team in a couple of days' time to assist MI6 in an important exercise in central London. Such exercises were normally carried out by A4 themselves, but being pledged to another job, they had recommended our unit. This was regarded as something of a compliment as only the MPSB had been used before for these exercises.

The circumstances were that four MI6 officers were undergoing an intensive course in London to help prepare them for a posting to Moscow the following month, where, although under diplomatic cover, they would regularly be subject to routine surveillance by the FSB, the Russian security service successor to the KGB which was dissolved in 1991 following the collapse of the Soviet Union.

The brief was that the agents would pose as sightseers touring the west end of London whilst under our covert surveillance. They were split into two pairs and we deployed five officers to each pair. Throughout the day, the agents would deploy routine anti-surveillance techniques to determine if they were being followed and to identify our operatives. Our team had major issues throughout the exercise with communications difficulties, especially on the underground, but it served to remind us that we could not always rely on technology and that basic hand signals and pre-arranged body language could work well if practised sufficiently.

On completion of the exercise, the agents and our team headed to MI6 Headquarters at Vauxhall Cross for a detailed debrief. The building itself was an experience to visit, having only been opened by Her Majesty the Queen in 1994. The designing architect had taken his inspiration from a combination of an Aztec temple and Battersea Power Station! It has sixty different roof areas, extends well below street level and is of course bulletproof, bombproof and every other proof.

On passing through the secure doors of this citadel of reinforced concrete, we were shown to a large, plain briefing room. I felt a surge of accomplishment; I couldn't help thinking what a long way I'd come from the young bobby in uniform who'd publicly walked into a lamp post thirty years ago, to debriefing four spies and a surveillance team inside the headquarters of the Secret Intelligence Service. Some journey over the past three decades and I wouldn't have missed any of it. Well, maybe just a little bit of it!

The debrief went better than I expected and although two of the agents had spotted a couple of individuals from our team, they were discounted as surveillance because they were not seen again throughout the day. Given our communications problems, I was pleased with how we did, and there is no doubt we gained as much from the day as the agents themselves.

The last twelve months of my time with Special Branch was also my final year in the police service but it turned out to be the most interestingly manic period of my entire career. One Tuesday afternoon, sitting at my desk in the SB office at the police station whilst wading through a pile of intelligence reports I heard one of the DCs in the office shout, "Jesus, no!"

I looked up to see him rush across to the television set in the corner and grab the remote to turn up the sound. The images we watched on Sky News over the following minutes shook the world. It was the 11th September 2001 and Al-Qaeda had unleashed the deadliest terrorist attack in history against the United States when two hijacked planes crashed into the North and South towers of the World Trade Centre in Lower Manhattan and a third plane was crashed into the Pentagon in Virginia. Just under 3,000 people were murdered. Another plane piloted by one of four hijackers crashed into a field in Pennsylvania following heroic resistance from passengers and crew, undoubtedly saving the lives of many other would-be victims. The intended target of that aircraft is still unknown but suspected to be either the White House or the US Capitol building.

In the immediate aftermath, MI5 was inundated with potential leads to terrorist plots and the thinking in Whitehall was that the causes of terrorism needed to be urgently investigated and in particular, the disaffected Muslim youth in Britain. In tandem with the security services and every Special Branch in the country, our work over the following months was concentrated on identifying and tracing possible contacts and associates of those known or suspected to be affiliated in any way to Al-Qaeda.

For me, that horrific day crystallised the reason for the existence of the security and intelligence services and why they must never be undermined nor underfunded. Those who would do us harm will continue to become more innovative in their methods and it is impossible to prevent every terrorist attack. A chilling statement issued by the Provisional IRA following their attempt to murder Prime Minister Margaret Thatcher in the bombing of Brighton's Grand Hotel in 1984 said simply: "Today we were unlucky, but remember we only have to be lucky once. You will have to be lucky always."

MI5 conducts around five hundred 'live' counter terrorism operations at any one time involving some 3,000 'active subjects of interest' as they are called. With finite resources, each subject is given a priority rating to ensure the best use of teams and equipment. Individuals who are not on the intelligence network radar will inevitably slip through the net, as indicated by Jonathan Evans, a former Director General of MI5 when he famously said, "We have to prioritise ruthlessly because we can still only hit the crocodiles nearest the boat."

Although my particular service with Special Branch was eventful, the department was to play an even more significant role in safeguarding the security of the country when, in early 2003, MI5 obtained intelligence indicating that an individual called Mohammed Qayum Khan from Luton was the leader of an Al-Qaeda facilitation network in the UK and that plans were underway to carry out attacks designed to cause mass casualties in nightclubs, pubs and shopping centres throughout the south-east of England. It transpired to be the first major Islamist conspiracy to bomb targets in the UK since the 9/11 attacks and became the largest counterterrorist operation yet undertaken by either the Security Service or the police. Under the code name Operation Crevice, MI5 and police carried out thousands of hours of surveillance and in March 2004 all the key suspects were arrested before they were ready to begin their bombing campaign. Following a year-long trial, one of the largest and most expensive in British legal history, five men were convicted for conspiracy to cause explosions likely to endanger life and sentenced to life imprisonment.

Many bomb plots and potential attacks upon the UK have been, and continue to be, thwarted by intervention from the security services and police; most are not heralded and, for reasons of national security or the risk of impacting on other live investigations, must remain undisclosed to the public. Having witnessed the work of the men and women of the security services at first hand, I have no doubt that major contributary factors to our enjoyment of the freedoms we so often take for granted are their hard work, dedication and expertise. As a Special Branch supervisor, I was subject to a high level of Home Office security clearance in order to be authorised to attend briefings with and by the security services as well as being party to extremely sensitive intelligence. Consequently, over my six years with the department, I was involved in many covert enquiries and undercover operations, the details of which must obviously remain outside the public arena and I feel immensely privileged to have been involved at that level in matters of such importance to national security.

During my final months of service, I found myself experiencing occasional mild chest pain which came to a head one day whilst the team was carrying out a mobile surveillance operation in darkest Hertfordshire. We were monitoring the movements of a local individual who belonged to one of the Islamic fundamentalist organisations and was suspected of being directly connected to a group of Al-Qaeda sympathisers, one of whom he was believed to be meeting that day. A team of us were following the subject on foot in Hemel Hempstead when he suddenly turned off and walked quickly up to the railway station. If he boarded a train, part of our team needed to be with him and I was a good five minutes away from the station, so needing to make some ground I began to run towards the station.

I was aware of a dull ache in my chest but didn't think too much of it, although as I ran, the ache became an increasingly sharp pain and I had to stop. After about a minute or so, the pain lessened so I began to run again, this time at a slower pace. But the burning ache built once more and after another hundred yards I was compelled to radio in to the Ops Comm and declare myself out of the game. The surveillance continued and the rest of the team took the target by train into central London where premises and individuals were subsequently identified. It was a successful operation and I was furious with myself for having to leave it so abruptly, but I had to get medical attention. I was referred for an angiogram which revealed a slight narrowing of one of the coronary arteries; I was suffering from angina but the good news was that no surgery was needed and the condition could be treated with medication.

Amazingly, the angina did not worsen and the only time I experienced pain was if I ran or walked quickly in cold weather and even then, if I remained still, the discomfort faded within a minute or so. But it could of course have impeded my ability to work effectively in some circumstances, so I needed to accept the writing on the wall. Including my time with the Air Force Department Constabulary I had completed thirty-six years of service and regrettably, it was time to hang up the handcuffs.

Everyone comes to retirement with a different perspective according to their experience and it's fair to say that a number of my colleagues couldn't wait to leave the job as soon as their pensions were available. That wasn't the case with me, probably because I was lucky enough to have served in areas of policing that I thoroughly enjoyed and which suited me at the time. The job instilled in me a great deal of confidence and discipline as well as perseverance and there is little doubt that had I chosen a different path, I would have been a far more introverted individual and more importantly, would not have met Lynda and had the opportunity to experience the joy of the family I have.

I retired in July 2002 and a major tick on the 'proudest moments' list was being presented with a plaque by MI5. Inscribed above the Security Service coat of arms are the words:

'Presented to DS John Dee, for your friendship and support to the Service.'

With equal pride, I received a coat of arms shield from the Royal Ulster Constabulary, two of the boys having travelled from Belfast for the presentation. Both plaques, along with one from Bedfordshire Police and another received on leaving the Regional Crime Squad, have pride of place in the conservatory at home. So does the unique mounted cannabis pipe, a cherished memento presented to every Bedfordshire Drug Squad officer. They all serve to remind me of a ten-year-old kid who dreamed of one day being a detective, and despite a ton of hope and determination, deep down inside, wondered if he would make it. Even lumberjacks make mistakes.

ACKNOWLEDGEMENTS

Heartfelt thanks to my wife Lynda for her continuous support throughout the writing of this book. Her encouragement and ideas were invaluable, without which it would never have been completed.

My sincere appreciation also goes to friends and colleagues who helped to provide some of the material and its approval for use in the book.

Printed in Great Britain
by Amazon